A Bird's Eye View of a Soldier's Experiences in Iraq

An Anthology of Poetry

David K. Revill

AuthorHouse™
1663 Liberty Drive, Suite 200
Bloomington, IN 47403
www.authorhouse.com
Phone: 1-800-839-8640

First published by AuthorHouse 10/5/2007

ISBN: 1-4259-1834-4 (sc)

Printed in the United States of America
Bloomington, Indiana

This book is printed on acid-free paper.

"Special thanks are extended to all the public affairs personnel from the Corp of Engineers and Task Force who contributed photographs in Iraq, with special thanks to Polli Keller, photographer. Because you were there."

authorHOUSE™

A Break in the Day

After months of seeing VBIEDs and IEDs blowing up
Suspecting everything to be a threat
Thinking twice about every explosion or gunshot you hear
Always thinking what is next.

The best of times are those times when there is silence
And the artillery is not firing,
There is no indirect fire landing on the FOB
There is no return of small arms fire on the parameter,
It's peaceful.

These moments are the breaks every soldier like
Because on these days, a couple of soldiers won't get caught in an ambush
Nor will indirect fire, strategically placed, take out some unsuspecting troop
Neither will there be numerous losses as a result of explosive devises.

It is days like these that are a break in the day
And everyone jogs a little faster
Everyone walks a little lighter with his or her stride

A Heart of Remembrance

Water wells up from the depth of the soul
The heart is heavy-laden, and it can no longer stand bold
Too many thoughts rip at the mind
Remembering a fellow soldier now left behind.

No more challenges to see who is the best
No more chants to get that weight off their chest
No more pictures with friends just before a mission
All that's left are memories.

A room full of buddies
Old friends and leaders alike,
Looking upon a pair of boots, a helmet, and a rifle with a bayonet
All the things a soldier carries with their Kevlar vest.

Worse of all is the formation,
Call to attention
When the roll is called, the soldier's name is never answered.

That's another warrior gone down doing their best,
It's another friend that we will always carry in our heart.
TAPS will never be just another tune in the middle of the night.
This moment will last forever, long after the tears are dry.

Admiration of the Morning

On such a day as this, when the sun breaks over the horizon
It cast a luminescent ray of hope
Wherever doubt has started to rise.

Such a light makes several statements,
And none can be hidden,
It screams about the goodness of life
And all the things we need to do.

It screams about a brand new day,
Where you can start out on your way.
You are walking and talking, and all is well
You are not bound and helpless, so the world is swell.

Since you can breathe unassisted,
You are well on top of your game.
You can talk, whistle, and holler if you wish
It is really all the same.

But this morning is especially great, because someone awoke to see it.
Just to see this sight is pure admiration, for you have another chance to be what you want to be,
And to see all you want to see.

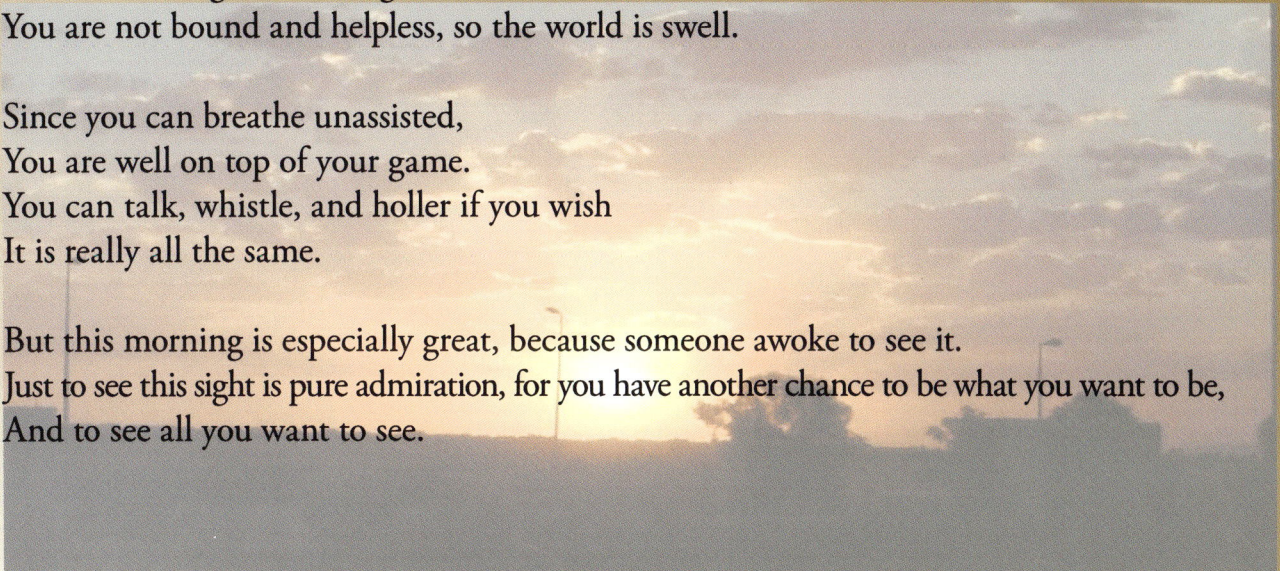

Advocates of a New Tomorrow

Many have stood their post, waiting for a better day
Sacrifices have been made that cannot be undone
But those who made those sacrifices, did it not in vain

Out of the midst of the chaos, peace will surely come
It doesn't matter what we do,
If the local population doesn't back the plan
There can be no tomorrow.

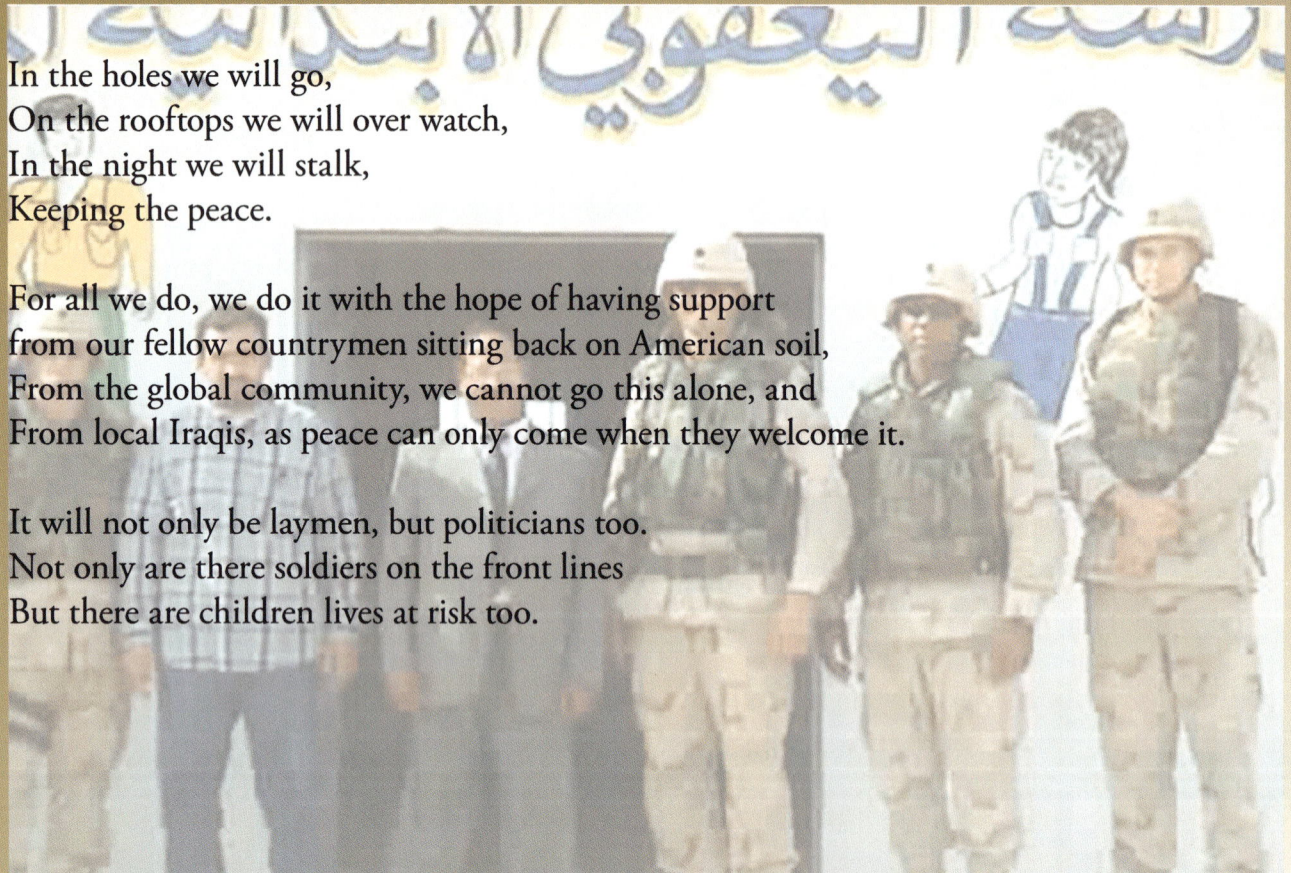

In the holes we will go,
On the rooftops we will over watch,
In the night we will stalk,
Keeping the peace.

For all we do, we do it with the hope of having support
from our fellow countrymen sitting back on American soil,
From the global community, we cannot go this alone, and
From local Iraqis, as peace can only come when they welcome it.

It will not only be laymen, but politicians too.
Not only are there soldiers on the front lines
But there are children lives at risk too.

Boys Today, Men Tomorrow

From the womb of a mother, birth is given to her male child.
Her wish? Let him see the day of his manhood and become a man.
She does not want him to get into trouble or to be consumed.
Let him be honorable, let him know integrity, let him be respected.

Riches would be nice to see, if that male child was fortunate to be.
Famous would also be nice, then everyone would know his name.
A role model would make him stand out for others to follow.
But maybe he will be a leader, not famous, not rich, but many would know his character.

What once was a child becomes a man.
The matter of not knowing quickly unfolds to see the man he will be.
You need not wonder will he be strong or weak,
He will be a role model, an image that many will seek.

Once he feared the dark at night asking for a li'l light,
But now he travels in the dark of night, hating to be seen in the light of day.
He no longer fears the unknown,
He moves stealthy. He is armed for battle He is ready to fight.

But all these changes did not come overnight,
They came through weeks and months and years,
Through a lot of sprains and many bruises
In the end the child became a man.

So the men you see with that flag on their right shoulder
was someone's little boy one day
Today that little boy is now a man helping another little boy have a better chance so he too
will be a man.

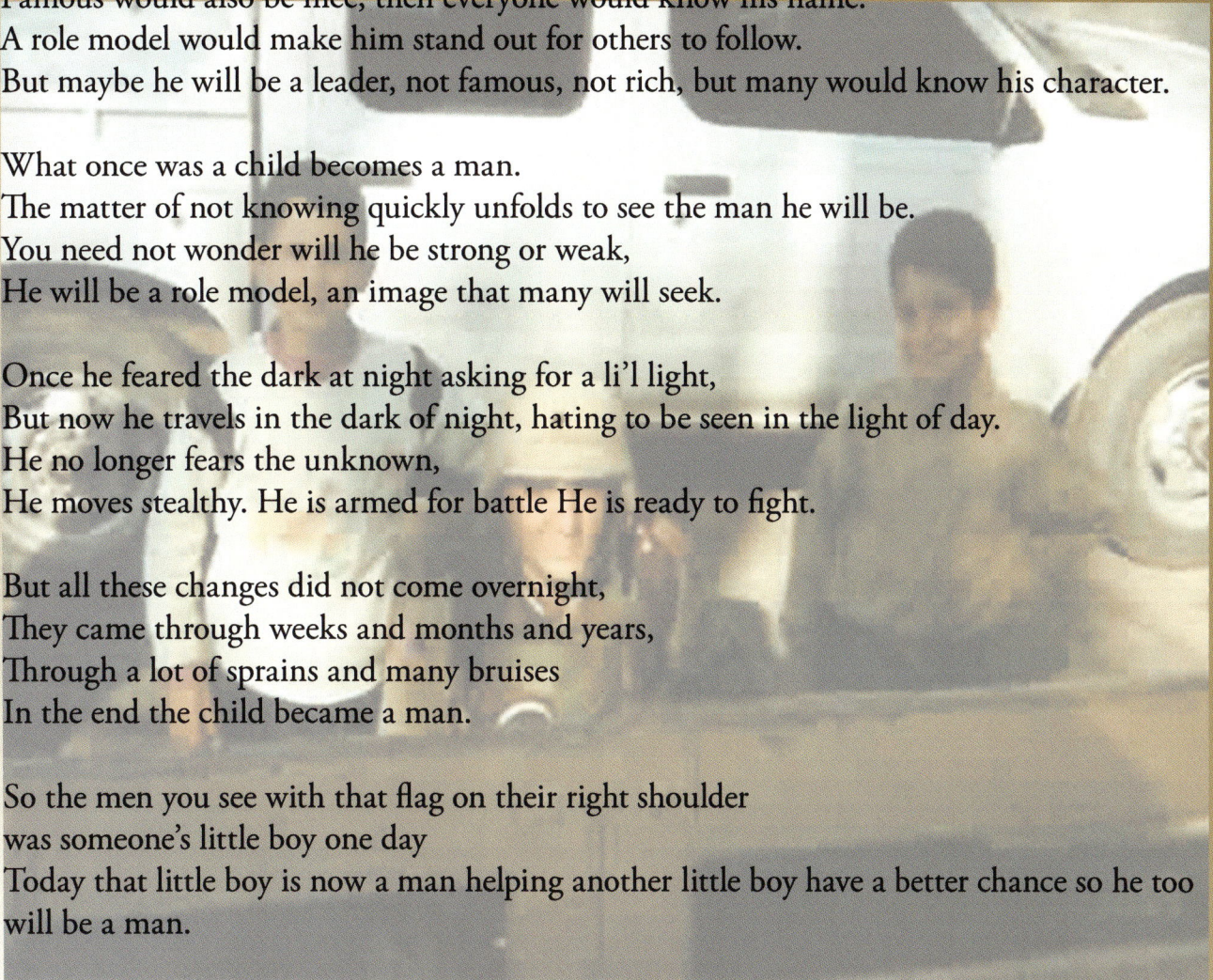

Brotherhood in Arms

We all understand the mission,
The operation order is very precise,
Rules of engagement leave no doubt
What to do if one of us gets shot.

Don't fire unless fired upon,
Choose your targets before you fire,
Discriminate in your targeting
Only fire upon those who are firing.

Fire team Alpha has security,
Fire team Bravo has the breach,
Assaulting force is ready to go,
A Sniper is hunkered down; the mark is in his sight.

We are all from one battalion,
Serving in the same company,
Divided by several platoons,
But our missions are the same.

One team, one fight
One army, one force
RDF is standing by with weapons day or night.

He has my back and I have his,
No slip ups, no errors
My brother is on point,
This is my family and this is the joint.

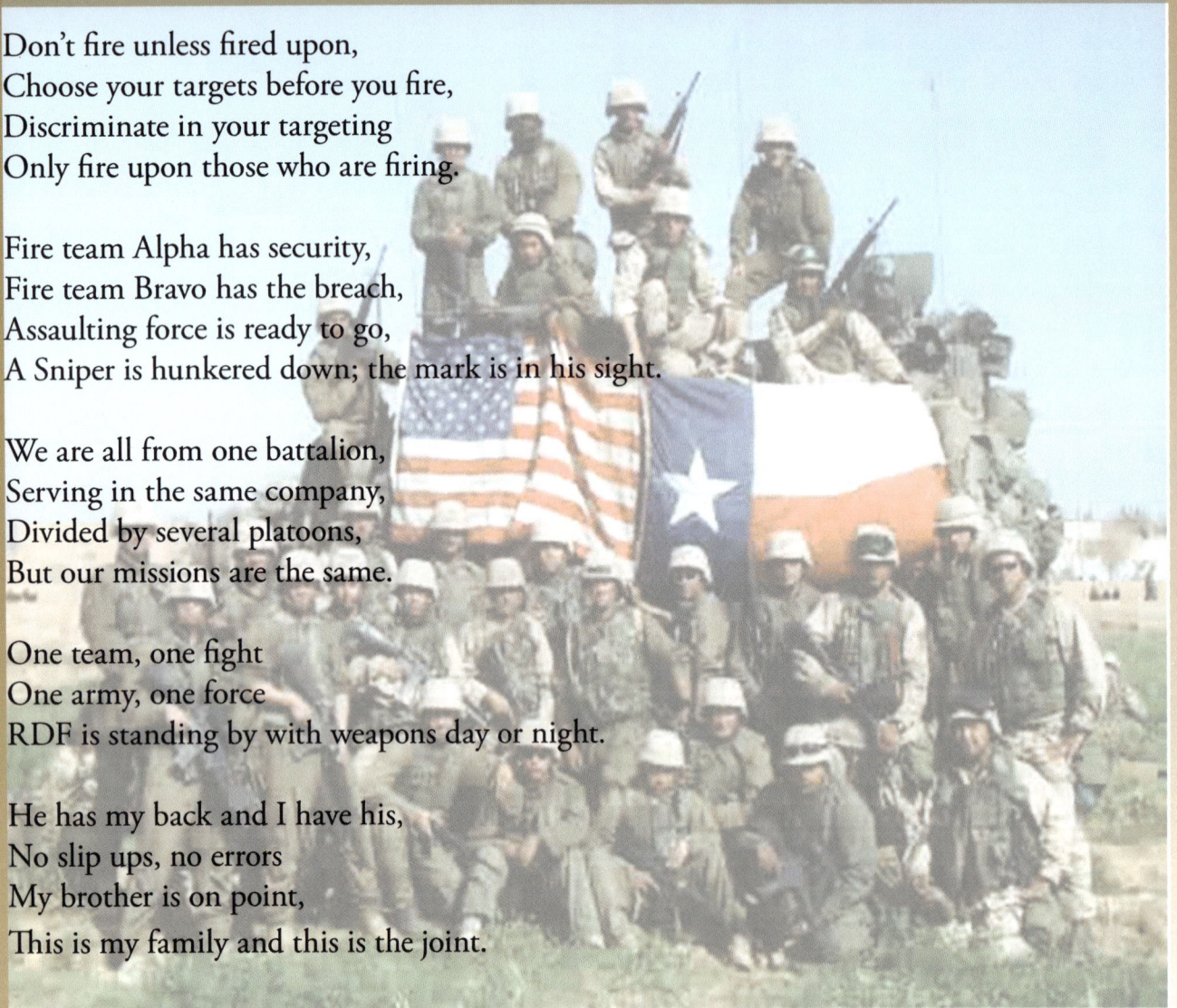

Building Hope by Empowering the Mind

Hope is not merely a matter of looking forward to a better day or a better tomorrow.
But it is also a matter of holding onto something within one self.

It's pride in self and self-esteem, seeing beyond the circumstances, knowing there is peace of mind.

Looking over their shoulders
they see so much grim and dismay,
but looking to the future
they see a much brighter day.

Tyranny is not looming over them,
Fear is not lurking at their door,
They are living with anticipation,
Teach me, their mind is open to a new approach, clear the way.

No longer need they fear to walk the streets,
nor fear that their father will not be home because of some scoundrelous rat who would
take a life simply because he could.

Bricks and mortar builds more structures.
They construct images of hope beyond the moment,
because within those walls and down those halls,
Tomorrow's minds will be built.

Weakness is made strong
Darkness is made into light
And hope brings to life a better future.

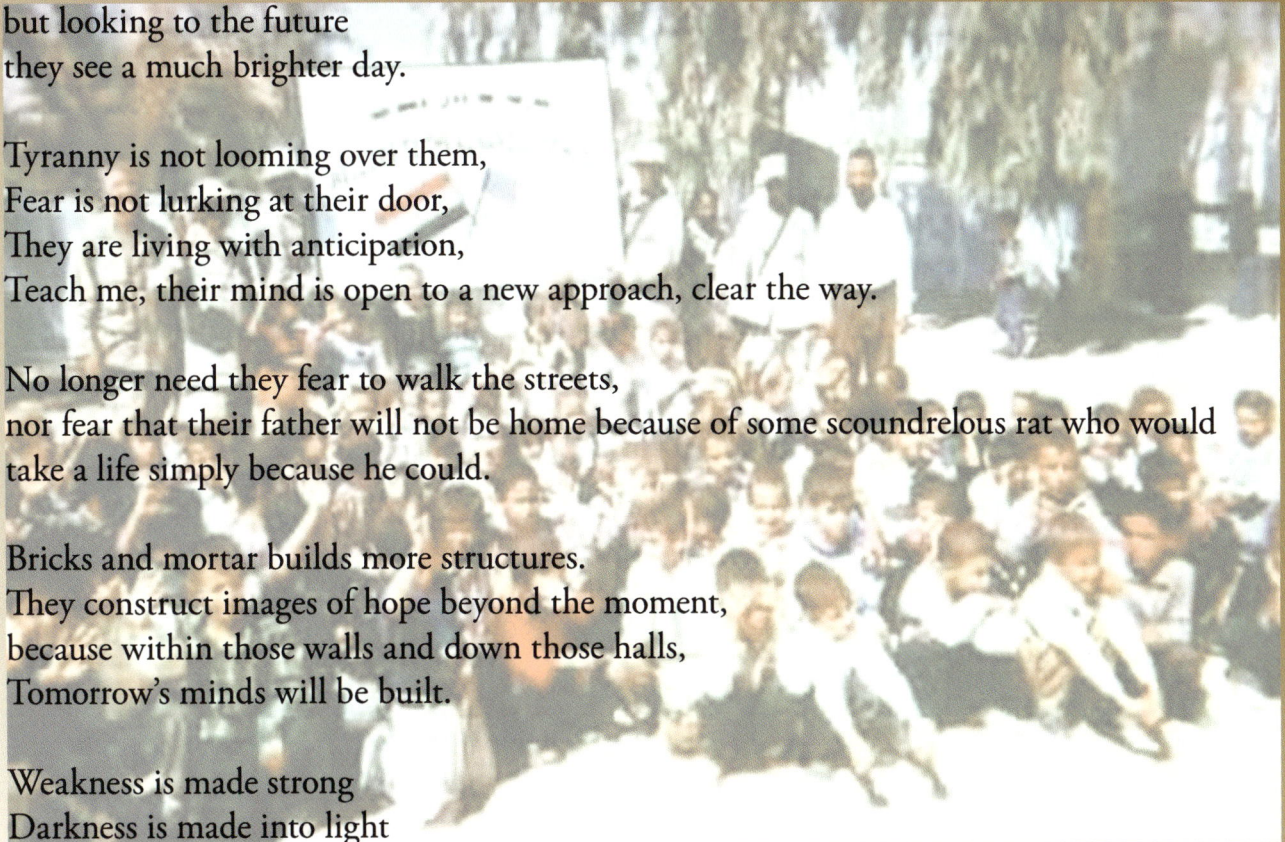

CAVALRYMEN

Who are those men who rise before bright morning nautical twilight?
And mount their beast of steel and bound through the early night?

Why are their beasts are so powerful and so fast? Are their gallant beasts invulnerable to their adversaries that lie in wait for them, in hope to ambush them at choke point?

Who are they? Are they immortal men of some sort or are they just super humans carrying out incredible feats?

They are not simply men; they are Cavalrymen.
Regardless of the difficulty of the mission, the task is clear.
Attack and destroy the enemy at all cost.

Is it arrogance they have? No, only self-confidence.
They are just battle-harden.

Have they traveled incredible distance, accomplished amazing feats or taken ground where others have failed?

They are the Cavalry, and when they were needed they were there.
On the wild frontier they rode gallantly to subdue impasse conflicts. They were there to insure that the east and the west met peacefully,
They rode along the borders to secure the line, and they were always first.

They are the Cavalry.

Upon their shoulders are adorned the largest patch of them all, but it only signifies that they have the largest hearts, the greatest courage, the most determination and the ultimate drive to succeed.

They are the Cavalry.

To those who serve under its colors they are a proud bunch.
When all else fail, they always have the option to "CHARGE", for they are the Cavalry.

They are the willing led by the greatest, forever seeking to do the impossible. Their legacy is world renown. If they can't do it, no one can. They are the Calvary with their Stetsons affixed about their brow they live honorably and fight courageously.

Charge is their cry.

Changing Minds

Little hands are attached to growing minds.
While they may be small this very moment,
They will grow up to think for themselves.

They will remember the good deeds that were done,
all the meals that were handed out, and the hearts that were won.

Those little eyes will soon mature.
What was small will then be tall.
Passing laws and making decrees
So what they see they will cease to be.

Treat them with kindness and kindness they will know.
Show them malice and hatred in return they will show.
It's just like an imprint; it will come back to our door.

For every handout,
For every smile,
For every piece of food,
We touch a child.

But once a child,
Next day a man.
Treat him right today,
Tomorrow an ally he will be along the way.

Impress their minds by touching their hands and their hearts,
When they grow older they will not depart.

Good deeds are contagious,
Do them and they will be done unto you,
Our soldiers are in the business of changing hearts
So that older minds will follow.

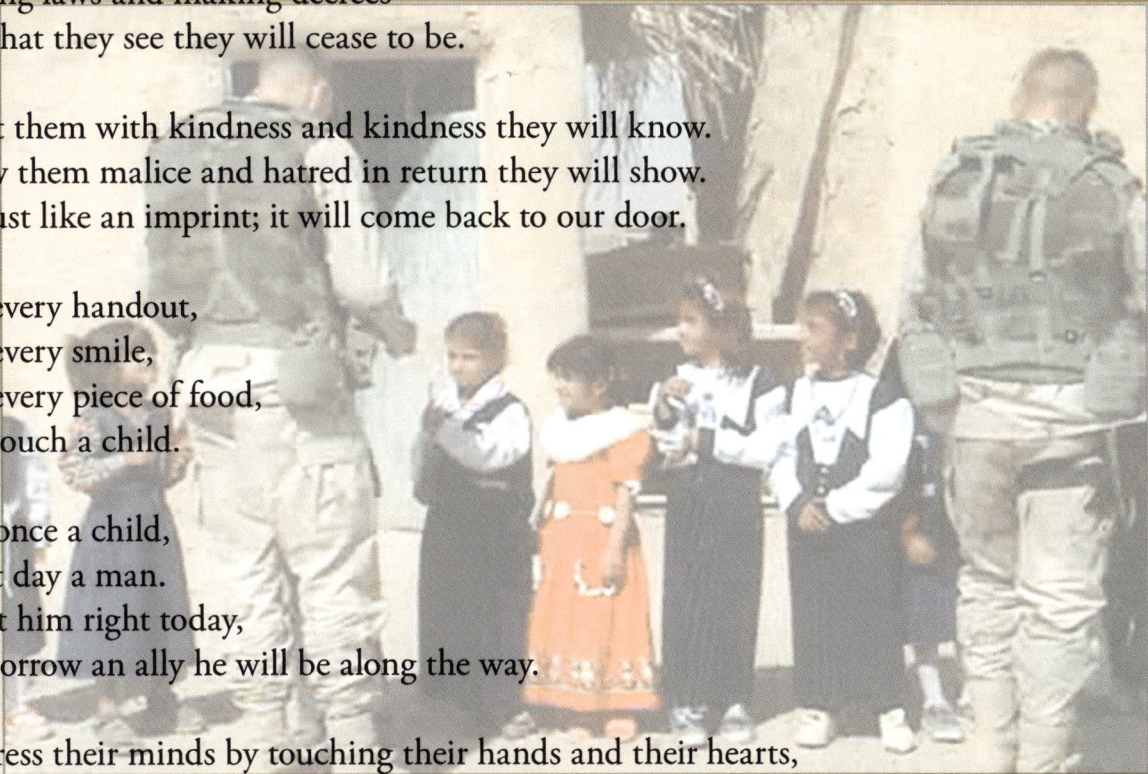

Christmas brings Healing

Christmas is more than evergreens and roasted chestnuts,
or presents piled high around the tree with ornate décor about the walls, or melodic tunes
filling the air as all the siblings fuss with their attire or fashioned hair.

The season of Christmas is more than running about the house, large or small, into the
kitchen then down the hall,
filled with excitement with not a worry in sight, waiting for that moment when from the
kitchen comes great delight.

There is a place where someone will have no evergreens,
and there will be no chestnuts to roast.
No presents piled high around the tree,
and no ornaments will garnish the walls.

The most melodic tune that they could wish to hear is silence
instead of gunfire, smell nothing instead of burning fumes…That's their wish for Christmas.

So to a soldier in uniform baring gifts of dolls and bears,
and girlie things for little girls hair; not to mention Tonka toys and action men that really
go wild when you wind 'em and let them spin, Christmas is more than just a season, it is a
time of healing.

Just maybe. a bomb will not blow or a mortar will not fire,
That will be their Merry Christmas.

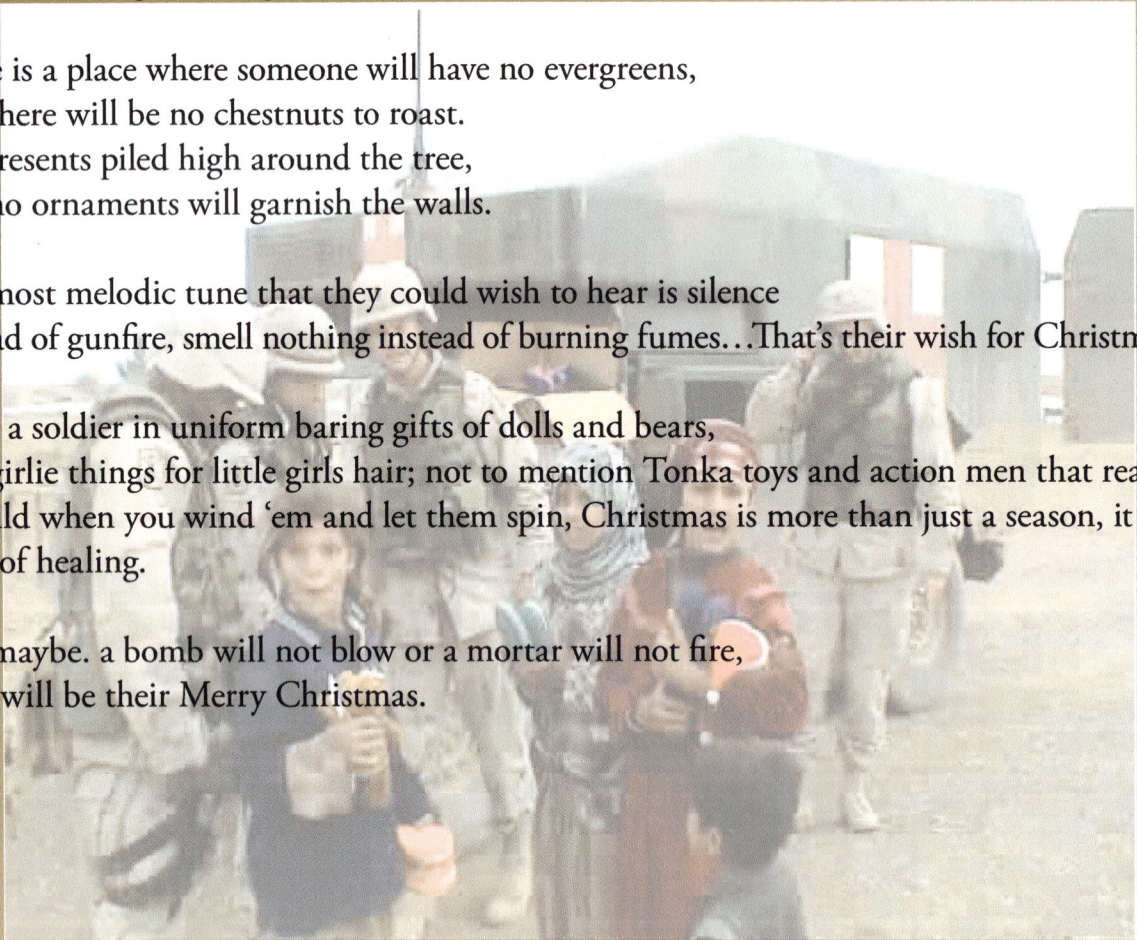

Circle of Prayer with Hope

Everyday in Iraq is a gift,
And every gift is precious
And everything that is precious is prayed over.

Before every mission and the convoy rolls out,
Circle the wagons, circle the troops,
Call one last meeting and let's say a prayer before we book.

It's no long drawn out prayer with a lot of fancy stuff,
just a lot of serious soldiers with a lot of serious hopes,
Praying that on this mission, just don't let it be the last.

Every soldier is holding the others hand.
It doesn't matter if it's a woman or a man.
All that matters is don't let anything happen
to the hand I am holding, and don't let anything happen to me.

In the midst of the prayers you see wet eyes dripping,
Intently filled with hope
Their deepest sincerity is, please bring us home whole.

It's only when the convoy is over, and all the members that were in the circle are together
again do they really know the value of the circle of prayer with hope.

Deny Not the World a Smile

Daily, you awaken gazing at a brand new day
Looking at the blessings that have certainly come your way.

While yet sleepy, and a little grumpy
A smirk painted across your face,
It is not in distaste but merely a moment,
For happiness is behind the eyes.

Around and about you move with grace
to start your day anew,
While you might be silent,
There is a smile in everything you do.

Into the day with a rush you enter,
the birds merely catch a glimpse.
But even they are enlighten by the look on your face
As they chirp on the branch of the pine.

Everyone notices a lovely smile.
It brightens everyone day.
But most of all it is felt the most
When it sits on a face like yours.

So smile to the world, and let them see what I have been privy to,
Deny not the world a smile.

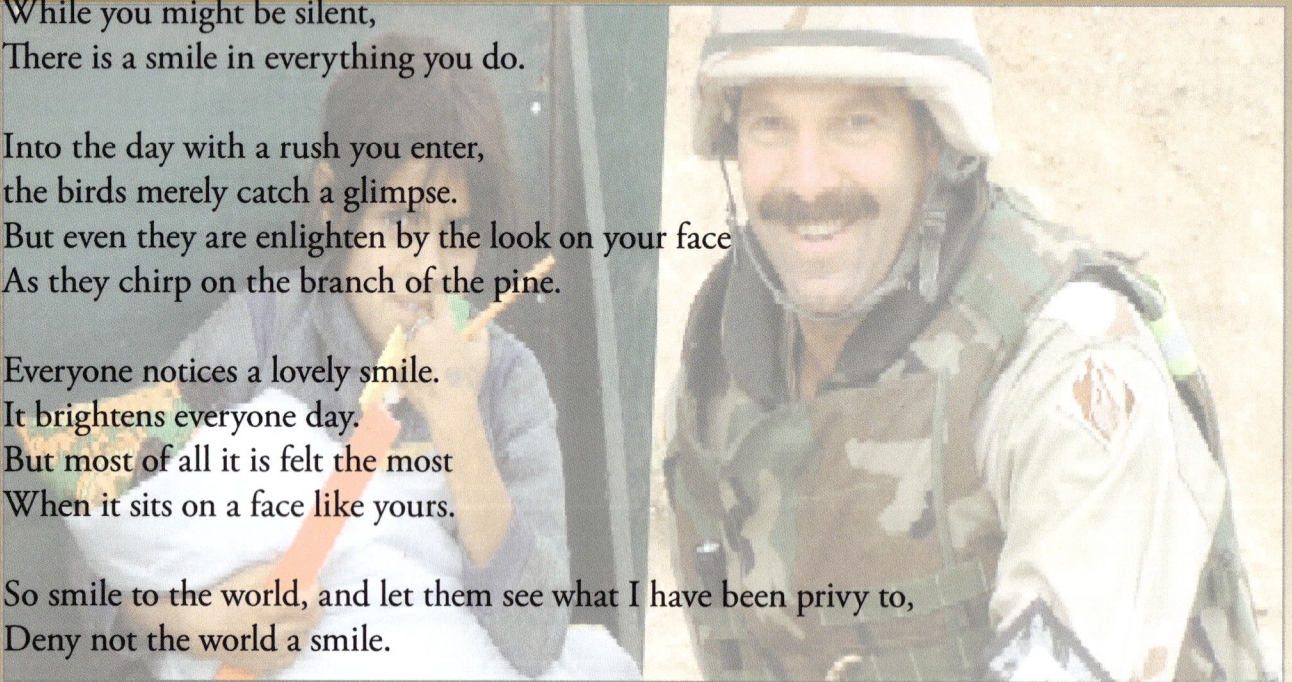

Emotions of Loss

Whoever said that men don't cry or that men are insensitive
haven't seen a soldier lose a close friend or someone under their command.

When you were just talking to them two hours ago,
joking with them just the other day, and now they lay sprawled out lifeless before you.

It was only minutes before that you heard him call for help, and later heard him cry out
that he was hit.
Now he is no more.

Men hurt and they have pain
They weep even if you don't see them, they do
The emotions of loss are greater than can be imagined.

In a brief moment of time, all sense of normalcy is gone because one less soul in your life is
gone that you knew, and cannot bring back.

Even Mayhem Has Lovely Moments

While patrols are moving out to secure key locations
And platoons are on missions to setup checkpoints
There is beauty in the fragrance from a blossom.

It would seem that in the midst of the chaos
When all Hades is coming down
That yet somewhere in some corner, love is yet abound

It's the crimson-like petals that are extended out wide
They hide not their innards from others to see
In full bloom, the world can see the extended anthers.

Even those that have started to wither
present themselves to be a gorgeous sight.
Yet in their death against the foliage
Their contrast is like light in the midst of night.

How precious the petals that folds onto themselves,
behaving as if they were royal ladies,
trying to protect their most valued wealth.

It is amazing that the eyes would find
Such an image that puzzles the mind
Even in the midst of turmoil, there is loveliness.

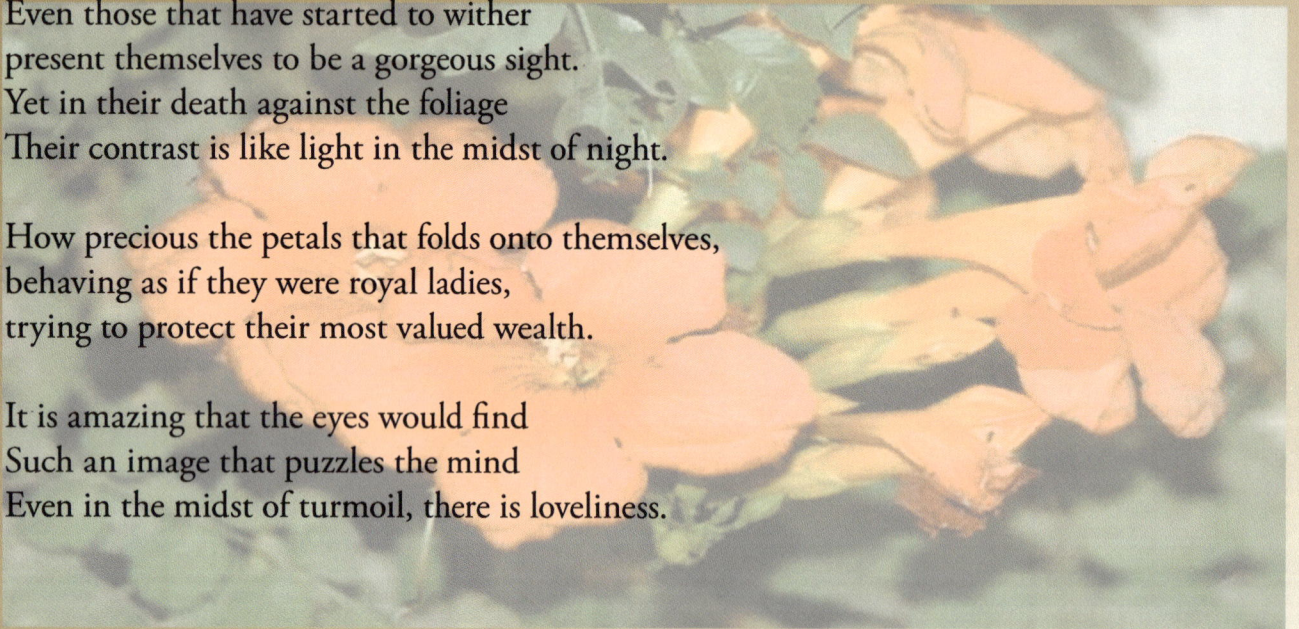

Every Hero Don't Wear BDUs

Veterans serve in times of war and peace
They are the first ones to go when the balloon goes up.
Back it up, they ruck up and they load up
And away they go.

They are the soldiers, marines, sailors and airmen
who serve in the armed forces to keep the freedom free.
And to ensure everyone can enjoy their constitutional rights.

But every hero does not get up at the crack of dawn
and run PT until the rising sun.
They don't march to a cadence of left right left to keep in step
But there is one thing they do that make them so, and that is their heart.

They feel for those who make the utmost sacrifices.
But more than just feeling, they act on their behalf.
They sing songs that are solace to the warriors' spirit.
They give of themselves to make the lives of warriors peaceful.

While they may never wear the name tag with 'US',
they are one of 'US'.
They are our heroes because like us,
They are us, feeling like a "United States".

Eyes of the Dove

Sitting upon its perch so high,
you have to wonder
what has it seen with those beady little eyes?

Has it seen an ambush
setup by insurgences with the perfect kill zone,
hoping to destroy many soldiers
and hurt many families resting back at home?

How many times did this dove fly over men fighting
for life on some dessert road, and it never once thought as it continued on its way.

How many lives have these eyes seen expire
that was caused by an attack when troops came under fire?
With a sharp vision, a keen sense of surrounding
They just flew away hoping to see another day.

From a birds-eye view, I am sure this dove have seen some things
That if he could talk, I am sure he would sing.

Faith Delivers Hope Delivers Peace

In the darkest hour where do you turn?
Friends, they run for cover.
Family, they are right beside you, but not in the same state
Social leaders, they are all for one and one for themselves.

So whom can they turn to?
Where can they hide?
Who is their refuge in such times of despair?

Is there not someone whose word is true?
Is there not someone who is not selfish and self-centered?
Someone who cares for the little ones, those who can't speak for themselves.

Who will speak of more than just rambunctious plans
without any intentions of ever making things better?
Who will truly represent something we can believe in,
something we can put hope in?

Faith is not understanding the how, but believing the when.
It's the very foundations that hope stands on, giving all who believe something to look
forward to.
It is in hope that peace is found.

When they see it, they know it.
Their faith is confirmed, hope is solidified
And deep inside, they find peace of mind they never had before.

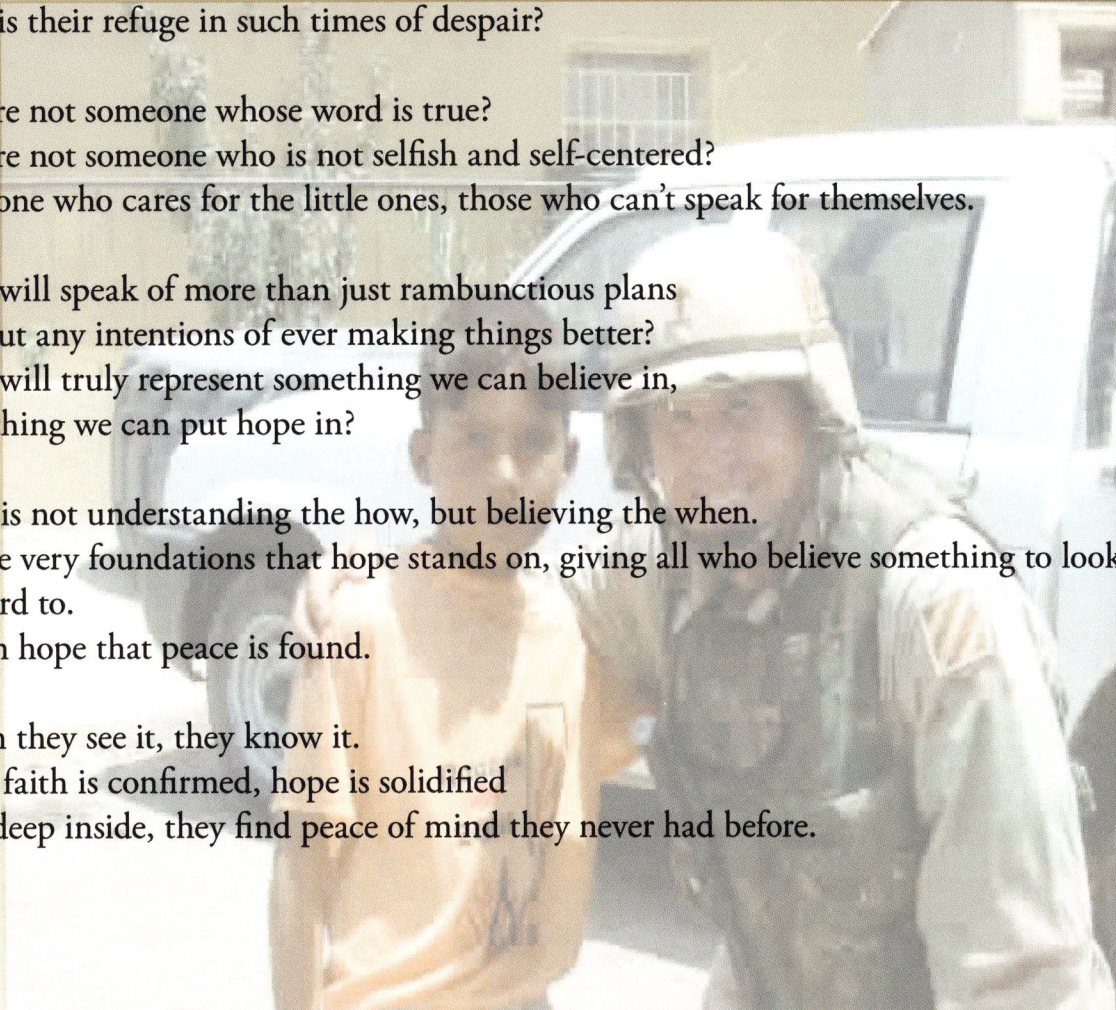

Fallen Tears That Won't Come Back

Before an assembled mass, we all stand to pay our respects
for a great comrade, a soldier and an American at his best.
Oh, what memories shall be recalled looking upon this time
They say this too will pass, but the question is," How long will it last?"

We have heard from all that knew him,
and those that served by his side.
Most of all the ones that last saw his chest rise.

They all say he will be remembered for all the deeds he has done.
What they fail to realize is that he was a friend of ours, and to us he was the one.

He was the joker during the somber times to make everyone crack.
He was the fire that motivated everyone to pick up the pace.
More than just a soldier, he was truly a solid-hearted friend.

We stand tall, but the tears just won't stop.
Sniffles are heard around the room and every head has dropped.
With falling tears that will not come back we all know the deal.
This friend of ours that we weep over, has fallen just like our tears.

A Family Lost in a Moment

What a difference one day can make to a family.
In a matter of 24 hours a family with a mother and father
quickly becomes a family orphaned, left with only kids.

Where daughters once looked up to their mother for guidance,
she is no more. Her voice is hushed in a moment of explosion.
The strong statue of the father, an image that was revered, has
fallen, no longer a vertical tower but a horizontal memory.

The sons will never look upon their father and mimic his gait.
They will never idolize his character and aim to be just like him.
The role model that he would have been in life, is praised in his passing.

The older siblings will be the voice of wisdom for the younger ones.
They must pass on how their mother was an angel to be cherished,
and how their dad was a giant of a man that each of the sons are to follow.

Their solemn disposition and grimness is based upon their love,
for the two greatest people in their life who will no longer be there.
Their smile is open to hope that they cannot see as they only have
tomorrow to look forward to; as yesterday is a memory they wish
they could relive.

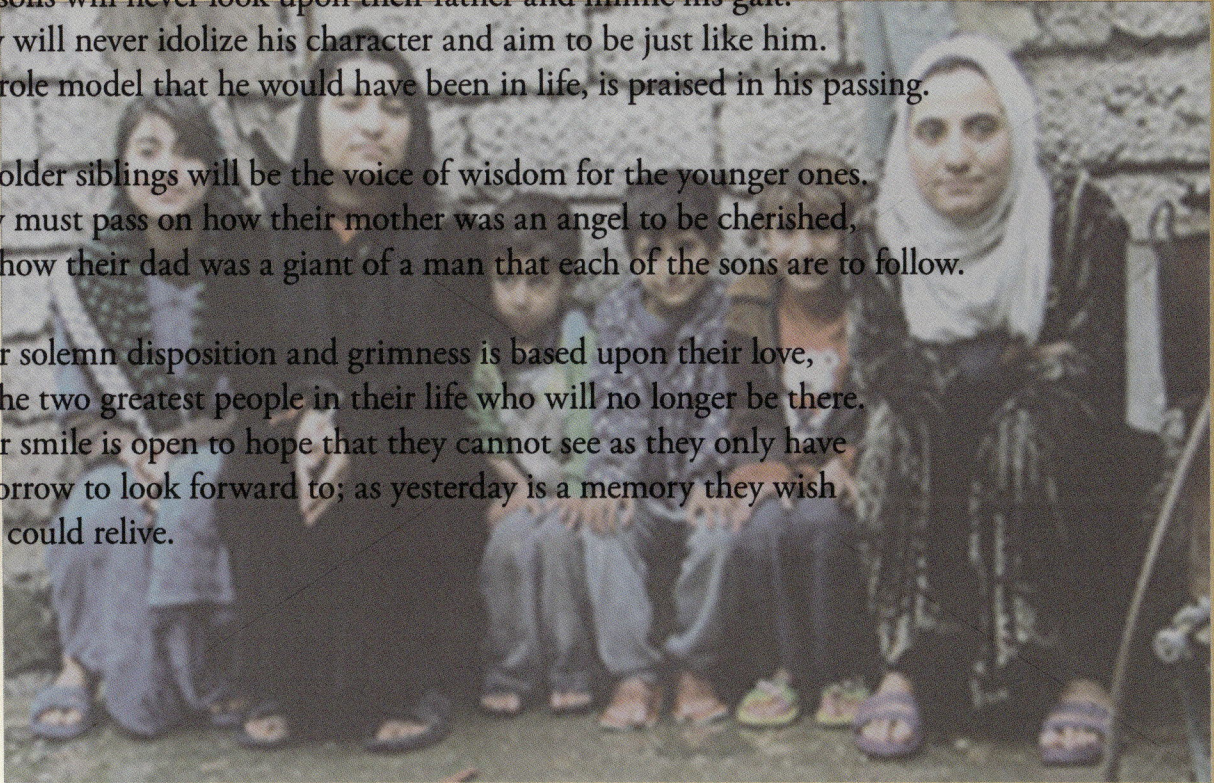

Fighting, Even in the Dead of Night

When the enemy is on the run and the fire team is in hot pursuit,
nothing will stand in that fire team's way.
from stopping tyranny wherever it lay.

Should the enemy run down some long dark ally?
Then so will the soldiers on their heels.
They shall not halt nor shall they rest
until they have them in hand zip ties.

No matter where the enemy shall try to hide,
our soldiers will be on their backsides,
hammering and pushing to route them out,
Wherever their strong is, no matter how stout.

The infantry teams will be stacked four high
Shot gunner up front, ready to take the door out.

Even in the dead of night, barely anyone can see the light.
Stealthily they will move to the door, giving their signs once more.
Bursting in and securing the room and to any violators be doomed.

They shall not be hindered.
They shall not be slowed.
Not even by the dead of night.

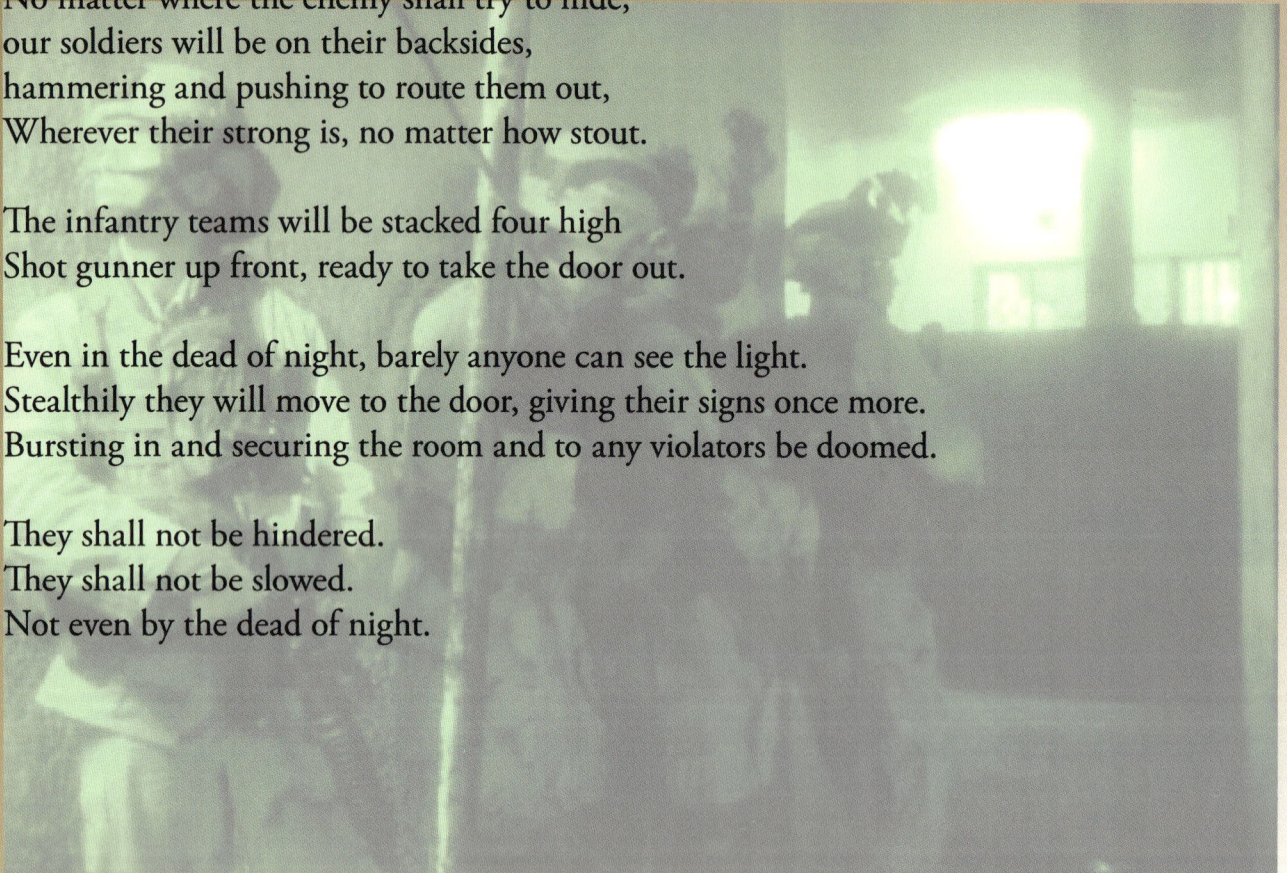

Fill the Heart, Strengthen the Mind

Where do you go when you are not strong enough?
What do you seek when you find your mortality?
Who council do you inquire in that flash of a second?
What do you hang on to when the thread of life is slimly divided by one breath?

There is no ranger buddy that can bridge the moment.
Not even the best "doc" can fend off the call of mortality.
There is no one that can tell you what you need for the moment.
When the thread is near its breaking point with only one breathe, you need more than you.

You need something that is not tied to time and space.
You require something that is everlasting without end.
Your search is for someone who can give split second advice.
Above all, you want a keeper that can give life as well as take it.

So in the moments when the bullets are not flying, seek out the omnipresence.
In the instance of well-being, get to know the chief surgeon on life.
In a pinch, get the best advice.
Lastly get to know the keeper.

Only with a filled heart is the mind made strong
It's all just in the nick of time.

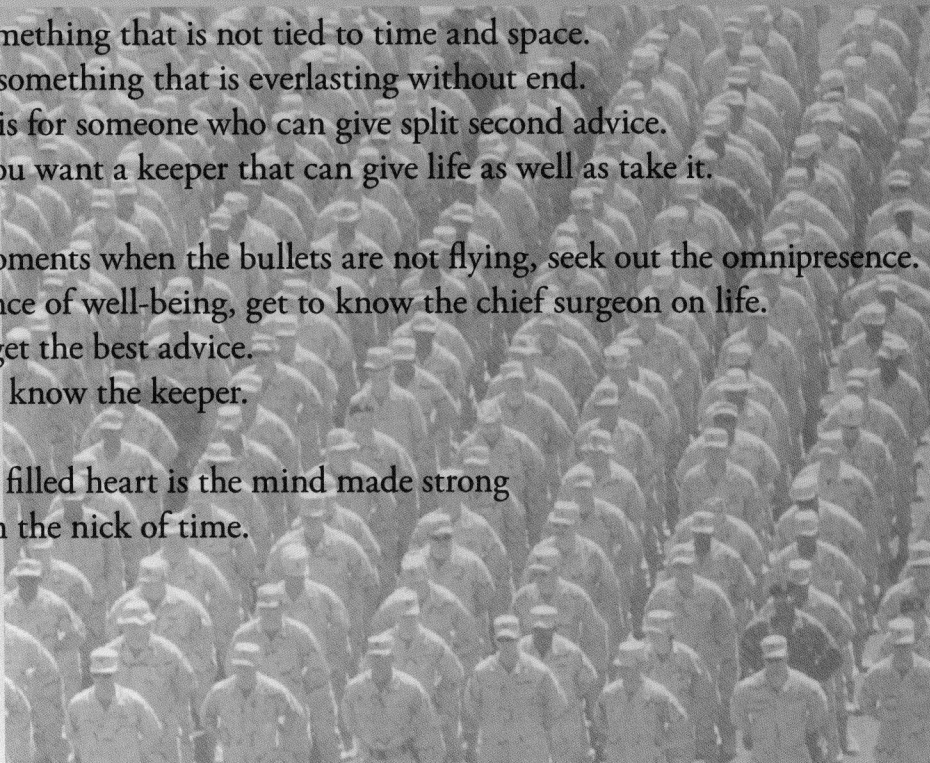

Freedom Ghost Rider

What a ghastly beast-like vessel it is
with railings around it on either side.
Sandbags stacked two high or more on the top
Just in case they get incoming, it will stop.

Armament extends from the top and the back
They are ready to face the threat
if those that dare will give it a go, it will be their last.

When the rounds are loaded and the systems are tested, and
commo is ready and online,
It is ready to hit the ally ways to see what insurgents it can find.

They are rolling down the MSR to setup another checkpoint when some wild bomber blows
a VBIEB,
But it doesn't hurt those inside, with only one flat, the mission rolls on, a Ghost Rider is in
the fight.

There are no sounds of tracks coming
to give their position away,
as they roll upon some bad guys
trying to make an IED along the main highway.

They try to run but they are not fast enough.
That 50 caliber is on their butt.
Another convoy will not get blown up
because the Ghost Riders are forcefully at work.

They are the Stryker patrols from task force freedom
And their nicknames are Ghost Riders
Because they are seldom heard but always felt
When they direct their lead on target.

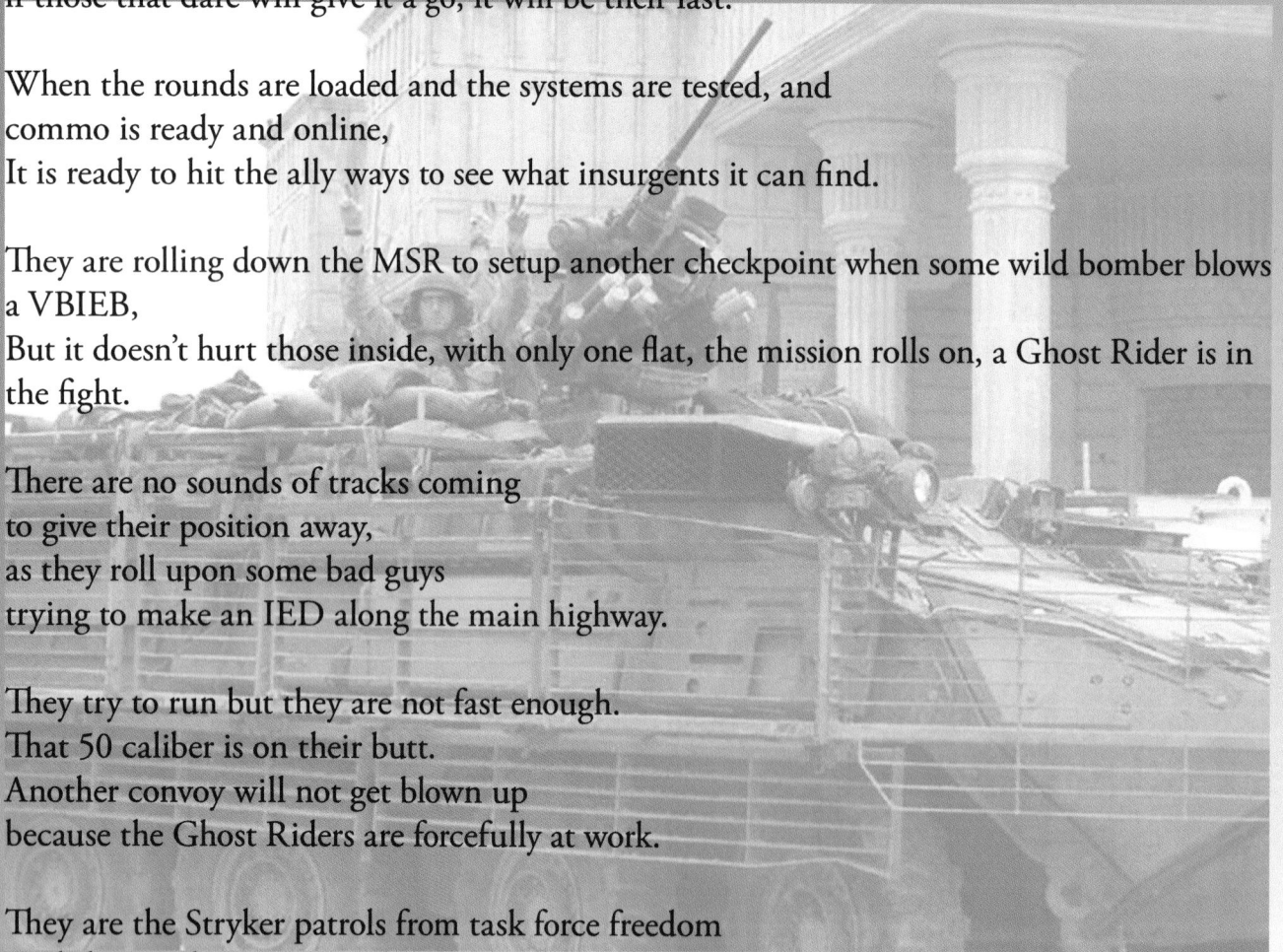

Freedom Has a Name

Freedom that is taken so casually by most is not nameless,
It is not faceless, nor is it without emotion.

It is reared in the big cities, developed in the hearth lands, seasoned by caring dedication and displayed valiantly on foreign soils.

While it suffers, it does not cry in pain, while it sacrifices, it does not demand recompense, committed it forges through.

Comfort is a nicety that freedom surrenders, discipline is a watchword,
Like water in the dessert, you need it to make it through.
Courage is the very push in the back to run forward rather than coward back.

It does not grow tired, nor does it grow weak.
Under the most trying of times, it stands to post at ready arms;
a stricken face ready for battle and it will take a dare.

Dare to save a comrade, dare to stand and fight, dare to go 48 hours without sleep.
It will take a dare

But in the midst of it all, there is one thing that must be remembered, freedom has a name.

They might not write about it and name them one by one, and they might not erect monuments in their honors, but freedom carries the name of every fallen soldier on the field of battle.

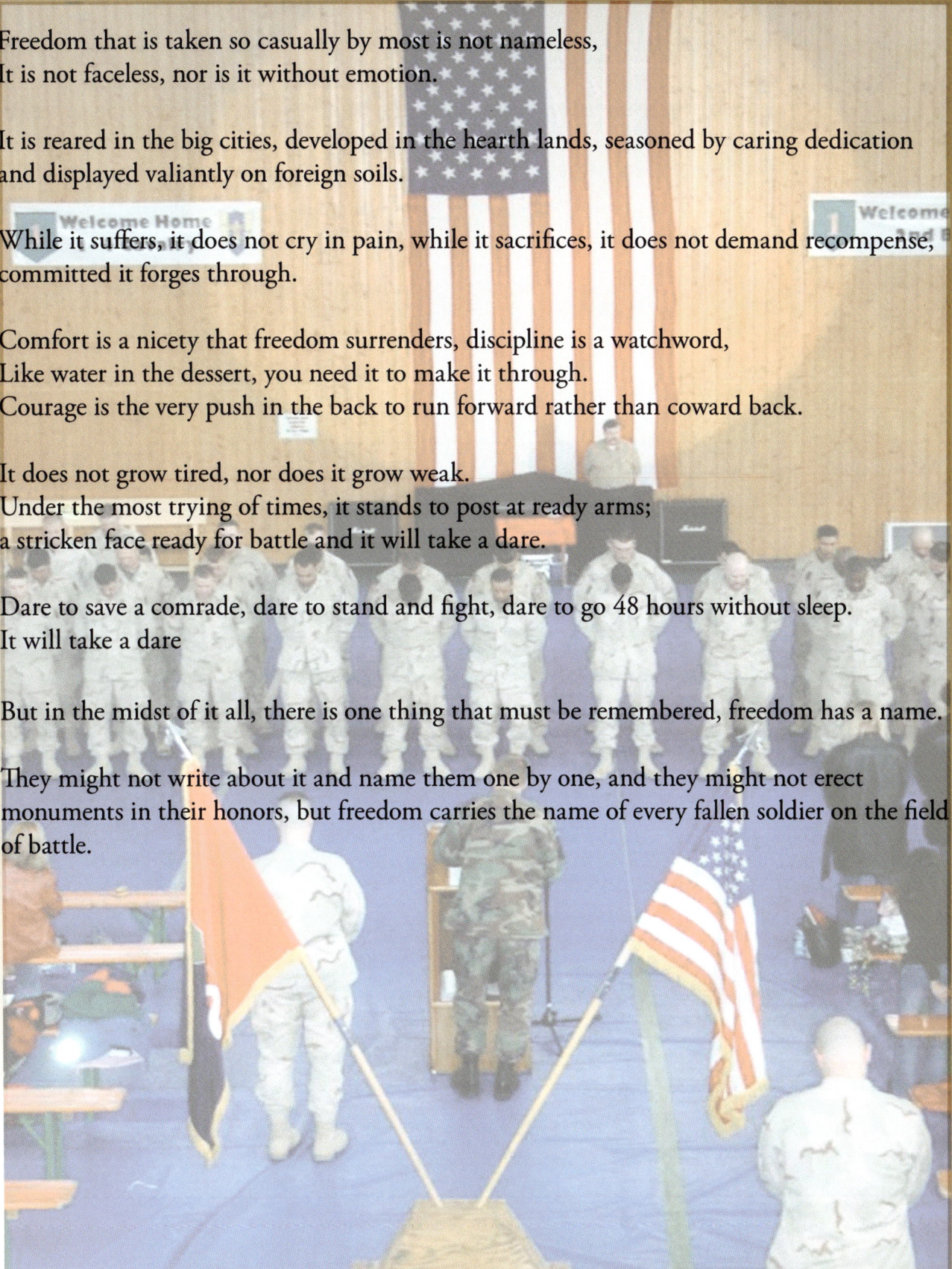

Friendship Produces Freedom

Friendship in its basic principle is where two people, regardless of their differences, practice sharing.

In the presence of each other, each member gains freedom to be weak, uninhibited to be happy, open to love.

Between friends, sharing become a vital practice if not a matter of survival. In pain, one friend opens their heart while the other reaches in with condolence and all feels the pain.

But also a friendship creates an almost indescribable air of freedom. All facades are removed, any superficial portrayal of personalities can be shattered…you are free to be you ….cry if you must, scream if it makes you feel better…but be free to be you.

It is one thing to be happy being one, but better when you can be happy with a friend. It doesn't even require words. When friends know the others' secrets, they just laugh….it is all fun.

In friendship there is a development of love, true Philos, that feeling that bonds two people…hanging together through it all, each one making a declaration "I have your back" and never backing away.

Above all, once found, friendship gives freedom and you can lean on the other, hang around the other, joke with the other, cry with each other, and in the midst of it all…. support each other.

Friendship does it all……my friend.

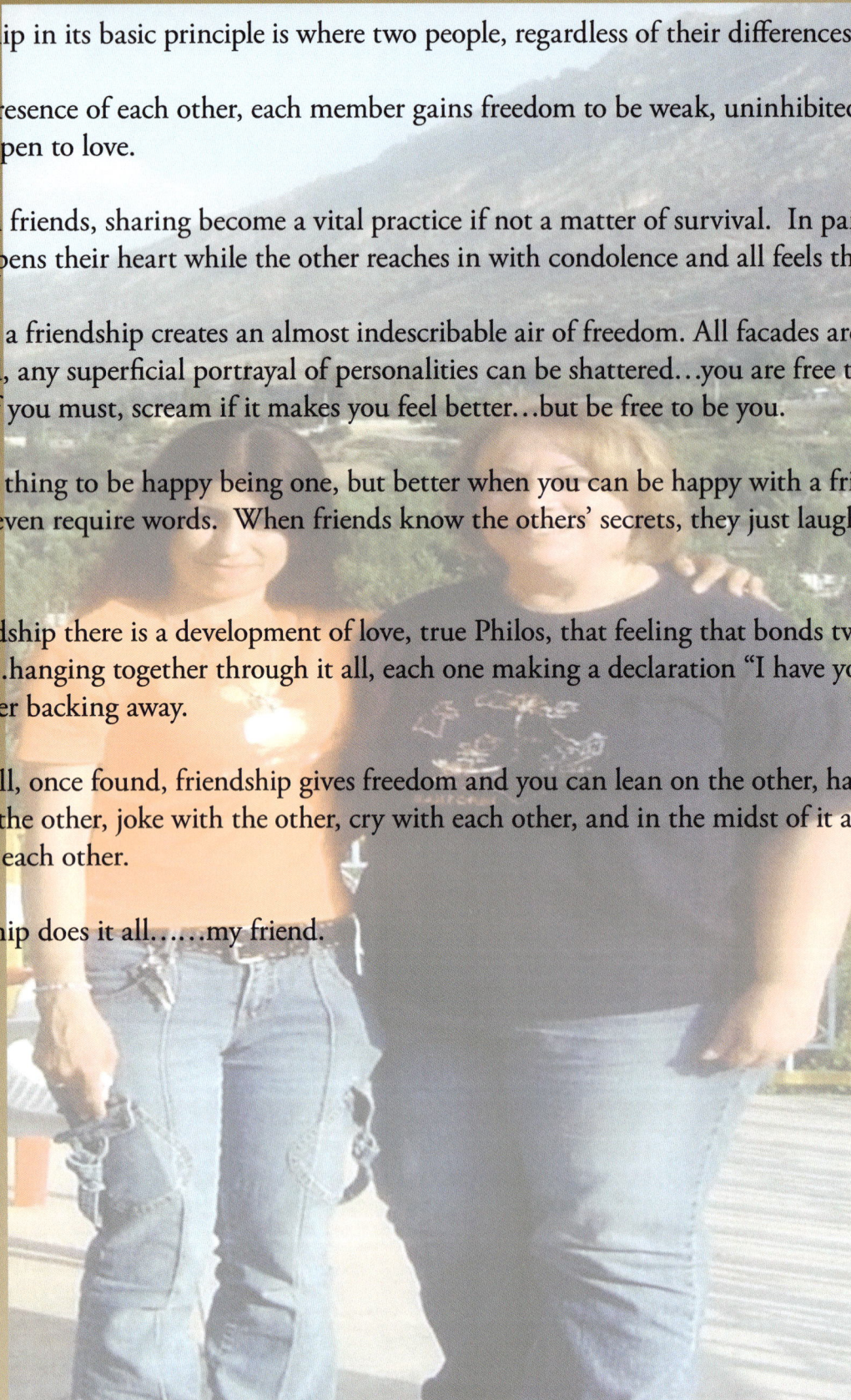

Fruits of Labor

People in the marketplace with produce galore,
So many choices to choose from
From eggplants, peas and peppers to melons, pears and tomatoes.

Each item in the market conveys a message of the labor it took to get it there.
It didn't just happen by chance that the harvest was so good,
it was based on the labor and how it was conceived.

Loving faces beam with life to show the root from which it came.
They were conceived from affection without knowing they would be fruit-worthy of the toil.

Much of the produce is robust, showing the investment of
healthy parentage and husbandry that brought it into being.
Not only was it a good crop harvest, but good young souls that will touch tomorrow.

The fruits of the labor are widely spread.
While the produces will be sold off and replenished,
the other will spout upwardly, able to sway the variance of hope.

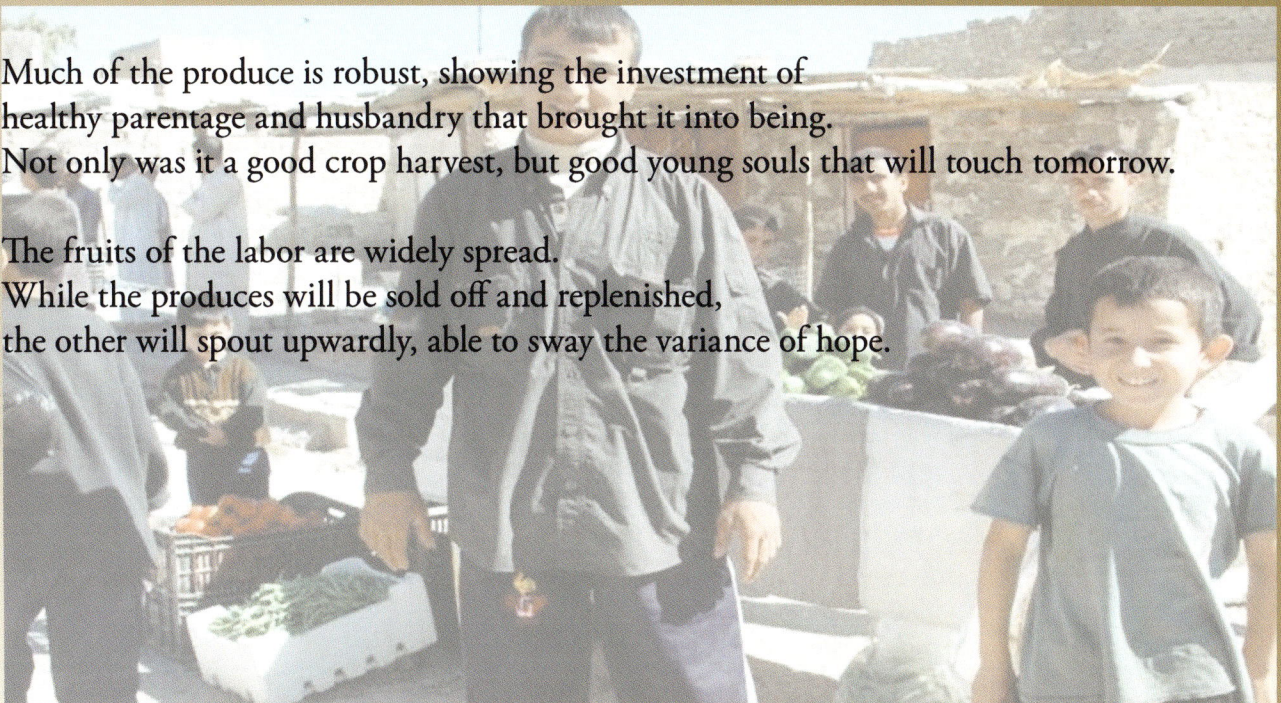

Every Tear Drop

The memories will never cease
Nor will the vivid images grow dim in the light day.

Just looking upon a portrait,
It is a mere image of the personality once known, it stirs remorse
knowing that the image will never be animated again.

We the willing, shall never forget the humble sacrifice
Of the most honorable, our comrades.

So every time we recall their falling
We recall how special they are;
Every tear is a memory; they are never forgotten, but mourned.

Futures That Freedom Build

What was it like before freedom?
What was it like when the streets were land-mined fields?
Or everyone lived in anticipation of what if.

What if there were no restrictions on what to eat.
What if there were no restrictions on where you could go.
What if there was no restriction on what you could be.

Everyone lived with what ifs.
But the what-ifs were merely dreams,
Inconceivable of ever coming true.

Only in the face of freedom did what-ifs start to vanish.
The what if they had something to eat was no longer, they had food to eat.
The what if where they could go vanished, they were not limited where they could go.
The what if they could be disappeared, they could be anything they wanted to be.

What was once bleak was no more.
Dark futures lit up like spirited candles.
Despair was replaced by hope.
Futures were rekindled by freedom.

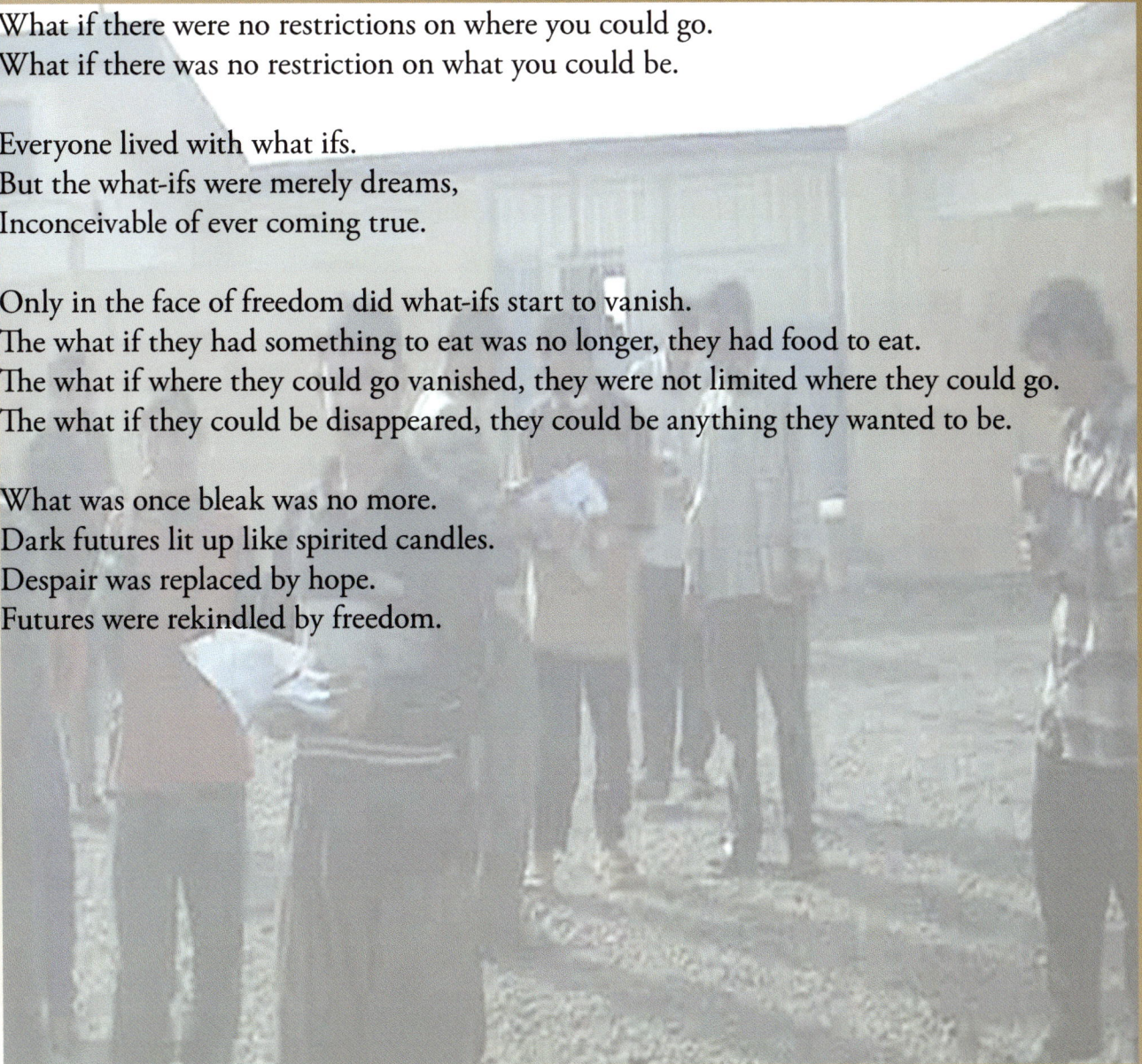

Gardens of Granite

Out across such open fields where sparse trees grow
rest memories of great yesterdays, knowing that they will be no more.

Through the garden gates wrought of iron metal leaf you go,
onto the benevolent grounds where simple men came to be immortal heroes.

Sculptured granite lie dress right dress,
aligned to the front and straight to the rear.
No wary botanicals like dandelions; nothing like that grows here.

From first inspection many would wonder,
Did the granite always grow like this?
But in the distance, a gathering and a 21-gun salute quickly eradicates that.

With a closer observation of the granite stomps
It very quickly becomes even clearer.
While it is a garden of granite, it is one of honored heroes, those that are long gone.

They are the ones that fought so valiantly
To keep the homeland free
But it wasn't always about their homeland,
Sometimes it was about someone else who simply wanted hope and peace.

So in this garden of granite
Where heroes grow like wild
Some little boy or girl had a chance to taste life.
Instead of them being in a garden, their futures are not unknown but hopeful.

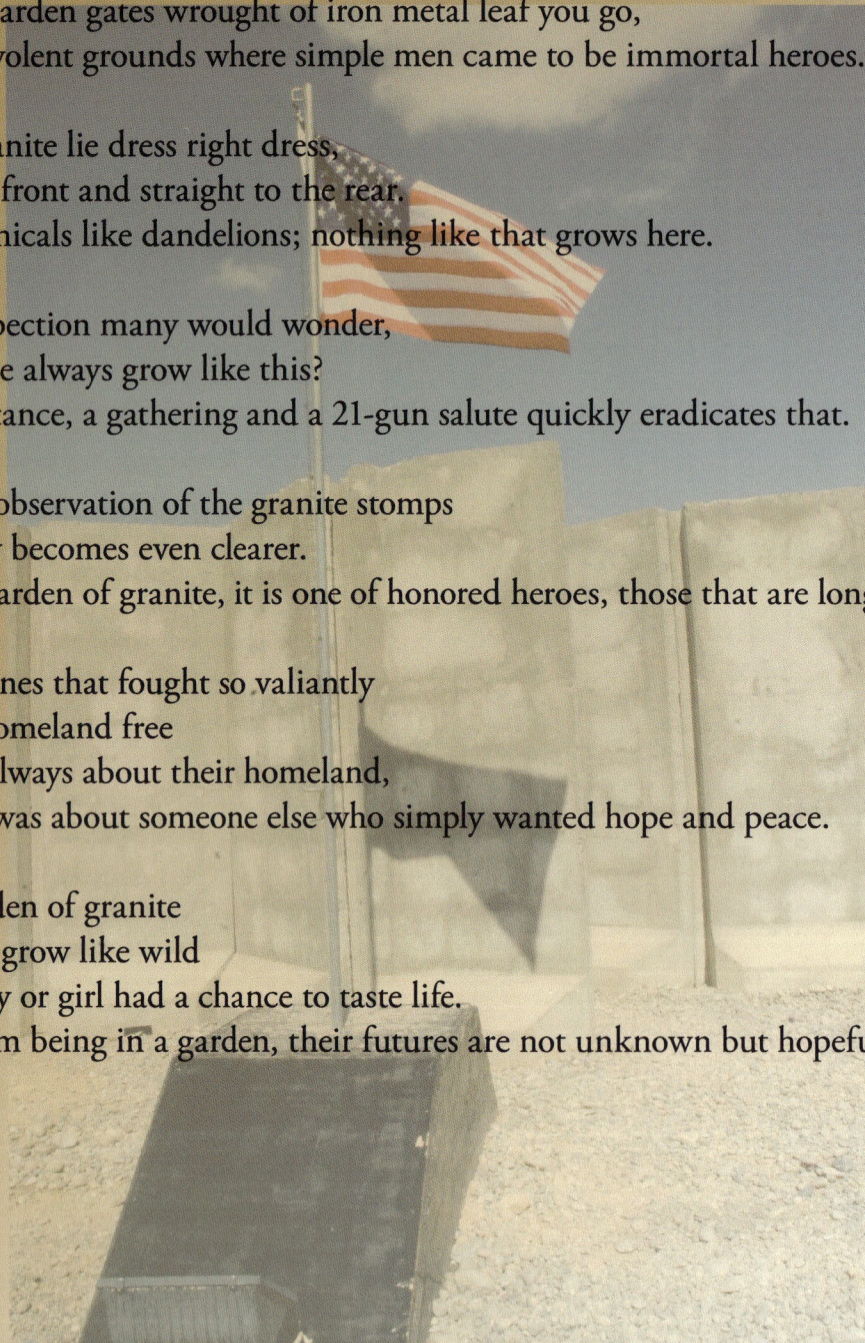

Glory Quenches the Thirst

Little dirty faces, tattered clothes, and hopeless looks
Seemingly no place to go
Empty handed, empty heart, and empty eyes just tears
the soul apart.

Nothing to cling to; where is the mother?
Is the father dead or near?
The look in the eyes, they are void without hope or fear.

It would be great to fill the hands with something hopeful
Even better to give to wanton fulfillment
If only a cooling swallow to soothe the scorched tongue.

For the very banner that symbolizes freedom
That has eradicated tyrannous regimes,
It waves on to beckon those in need
And give hope to the despair.

Hold it high; hold it on the right side.
Let those that support it fill your left hand with your needs…let glory quench your thirst.

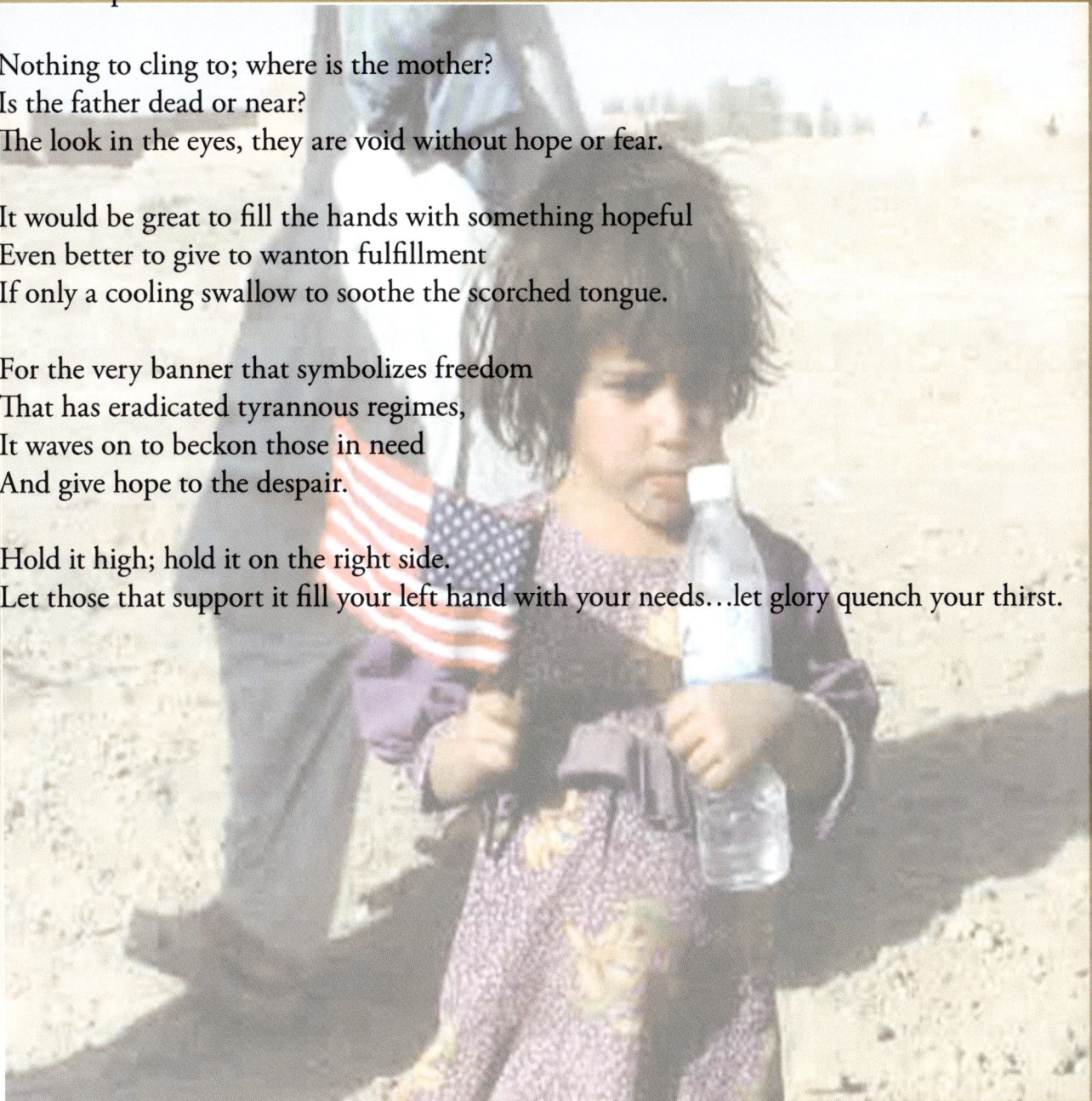

Golden Locks in Iraq

In a country so wrought with violence
And a people so surrounded by grief
The innocence stands out like crimson rose
against an opaque backdrop.

A face so young that it cannot understand why
A twinkle as azure as an empty western sky
With a look that is so captivating that just to look
Makes the heart cries.

What a capture of the moment,
How will her little life be
Hopefully we can make a difference
And this moment in her life will be more like a dream than a reality.

Golden locks in the mountains of Iraq
may your future be pleasant and bright.
May our presence in your country make
your future better and your smile wider.

Just to look upon her small modeled facial profile
There is so much depth, so much hope
Yet so much despair, she is almost an angel with golden hair.

When time looks back and sees her face
May it see only what she used to be
And not what she still is, the golden locks in Iraq.

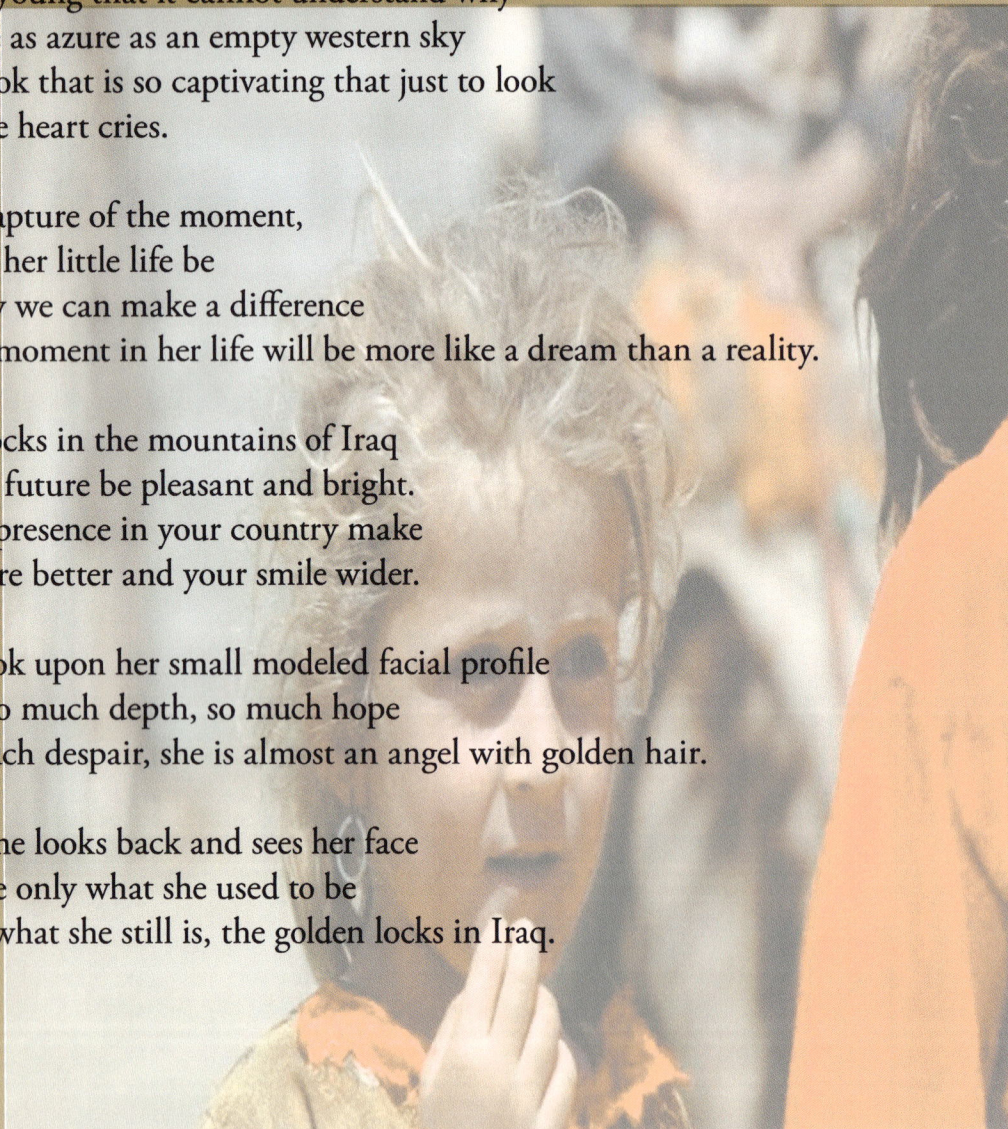

What Greater Love?

Some say they love their country
Others say they love their fellow man
While yet others claim their undying devotion
to help the good of man.

How cheap are words, they cost nothing.
The worth of those words are the true meaning.
There you find where the heart really is,
its true intention.

Daily, men and women asking for nothing in return
enter battle zones knowing the woes and chances they take.
Yet they place their gifts on the table, sparing someone else's
What a heart, what a sacrifice.

Forgetting all those who love them,
All the things that they have or ever wanted
All the dreams and imaginations.

When that moment encroaches upon them,
Courageously, distinguished, wishing to stay
They peacefully show their affection for their commitment.

They do not live by words undefined.
They walk their talk, living in action.
In the end, it is by their lives that they
make a broad statement, what greater Love.

Giving a Few Good Men

As the war on global terrorism thrives,
And soldiers are called to serve,
It requires the dedication of a few good men.

Men is not about a gender
But about a mentality
It is a set frame of mind
To seven distinct principles.

There is duty, doing the job
weathering the storm,
going the distance, and
knowing it's about a team, not a person.

The code of conduct is the measuring stick.
We live in honor, never to let our buddies down.
They are our comrades and our strength
And we are they're.

No one or thing is greater than a fellow soldier
Loyalty is our watchword and keeper.
Being true to the Corps, the institution and us.
If one falls, we all fall. Therefore, no one can fall. We stand together.

In the eyes of my fellow comrades I see myself.
And what I see is not a color, not a gender or race.
We are equal; no one body is greater than the next.
With respect, we are our brothers' keeper.

In truth we face our fears, our darkest most heinous phobias.
We hold our fear inward standing strong
But in the face of questions, we will be true
We must be forthright.

For all the fears that are contained
And all the doubts struggling inside,
there is a personal identity, an image of courage.
Even if we fall, we will go. We cannot stop.

And when the time is come to do my job
We will not shirk, stand at arms we will.
Willing to pay the cost.
If my cost will save another, let my price be paid selflessly.

Happy Faces

Where was the laughter when tyranny reigned?
Was there glittering ivory when everyone was forced to live without?
Is this something new or just a repressed action waiting to get out?

Every child should know what it is to smile
They should know laughter and how it feels to be carefree.
Every child should feel free to be just that, a child.

Let them not be burdened down with thoughts of shall they see another day.
Forbid them to fear if their lives are at risk if they exit the house.
How dare that they should ever have to worry about youth being stolen from them.

Remove the burden concerned about seeing another day.
Let them never know the fear of not being able to exit their homes.
Let fond memories be had of their childhood, not nightmares that are relived everyday for the rest of their lives.

Smiles on children faces or signs of images of horror are a distant memory.

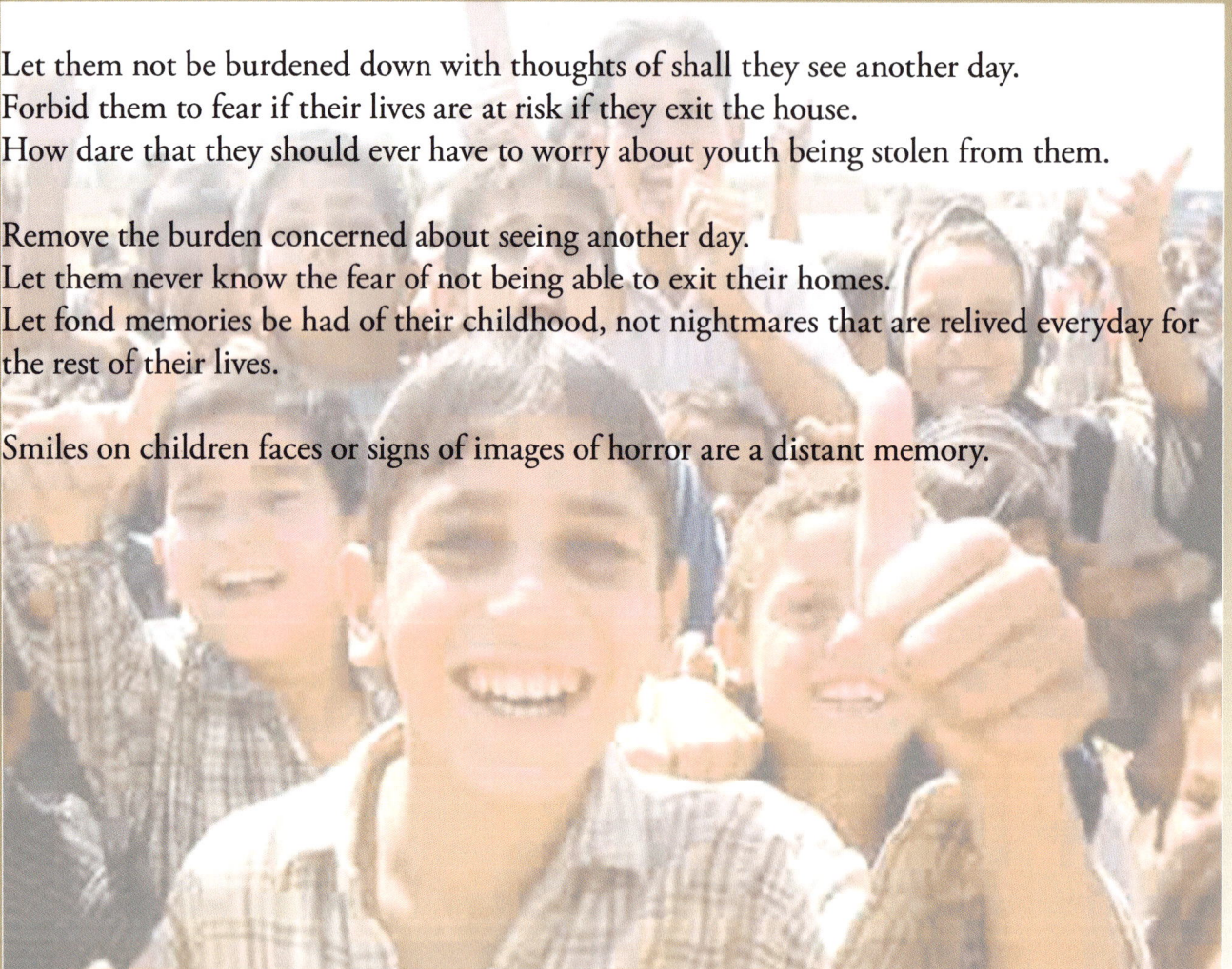

Heal the Heart; Heal the Nation

It's amazing what a caring touch can do.
It can help the lame to walk again.
Or prevent the furtherance of disease in an infant.
It has the power to restore health.

To those who are impoverished and in despair
Looking for a hand that is helping, not beating, that care
A single touch, a hand of hope can do so much, so cut the yoke.

In a strange land where the hand comes from new people,
Those in need question their motives.
As if to say, "What do they want?", "Is this a trick?"
All these questions initially run through their minds.

The hands that reach out to help a mother in need
Helping her find food for her children, and vitamins so that they can see, as well as finding
shoes for their feet so they will have a better chance to succeed.

What seems so simple and all in a days work
Is a miracle to those in need and that have been living in a rut.
Because the only hand they ever knew was the one that beat
Until they meet the one who offers to heal.

A helping hand not only mends the wounded and broken hearted,
but it changes the mind, and brings together that which is divided.
A nation once divided by hate is now healed by a touch.

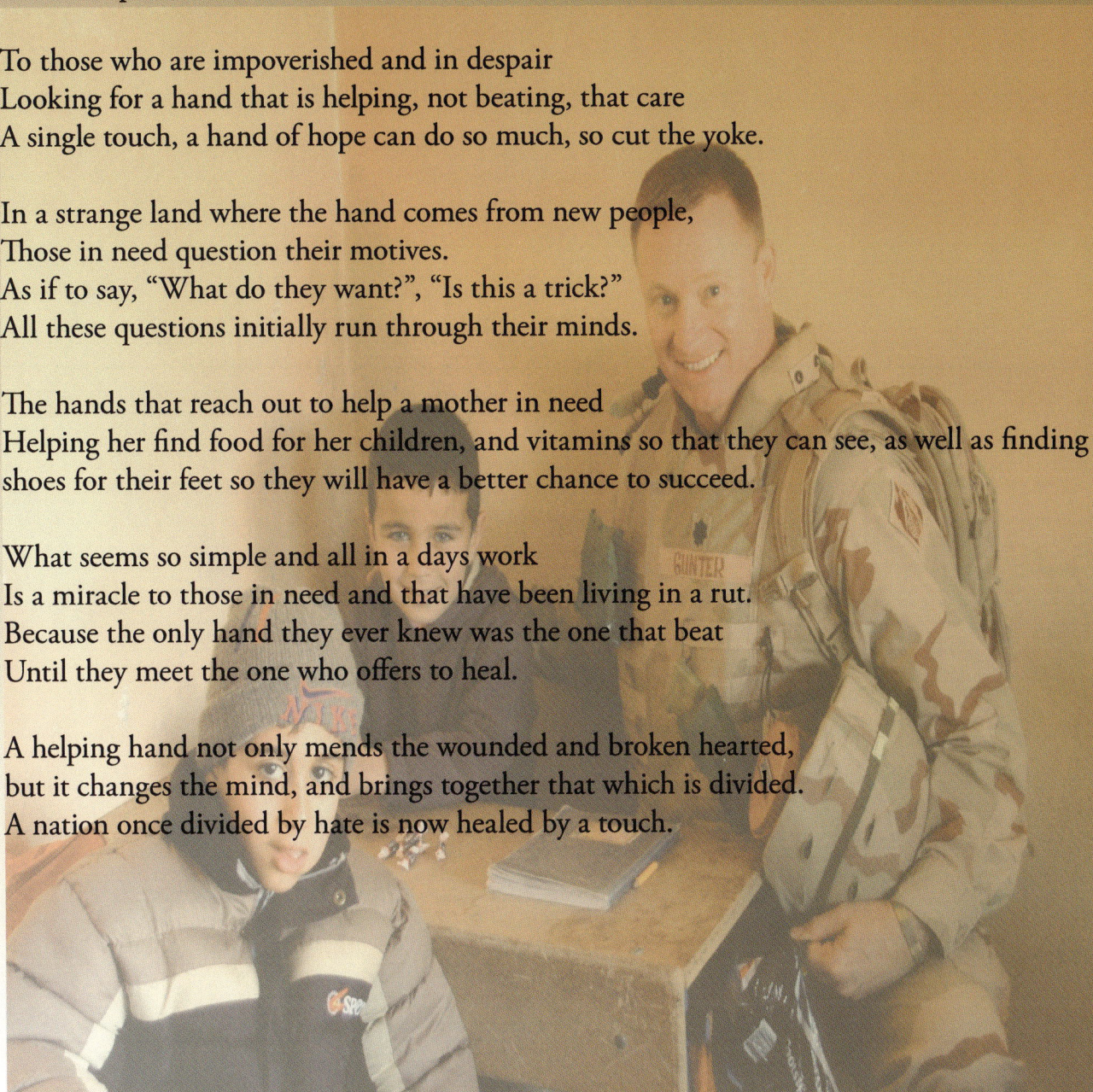

Heal Today, Save Tomorrow

The innocent, young, and influenced does not know
What the ruckus is all about. They only hear sounds.
They cry when they are hungry and,
they scream when they are in pain.

When it is cold outside and they are too,
their outbursts and persistence is an alert to how ill they are
and it is the mother who immediately feels the need to comfort.

The mother is more than willing to surrender her all
To see that her child is kept warm and healthy and
ultimately from all harm and danger even at the expense of her own life.

So when a strange face appears with a helping hand
Offering to help her child, the mother is most willing
If only the child can be healed today, it will be saved tomorrow.

With a medic bag in tow and goodies to show, that stranger comes bringing hope and
another chance to the child that might not have made it, and whose mother was worried.

Once again with more than rounds and weapons,
offensive operations and ambushes, but with smiles and
medicine, a child has been saved and tomorrow is made brighter.

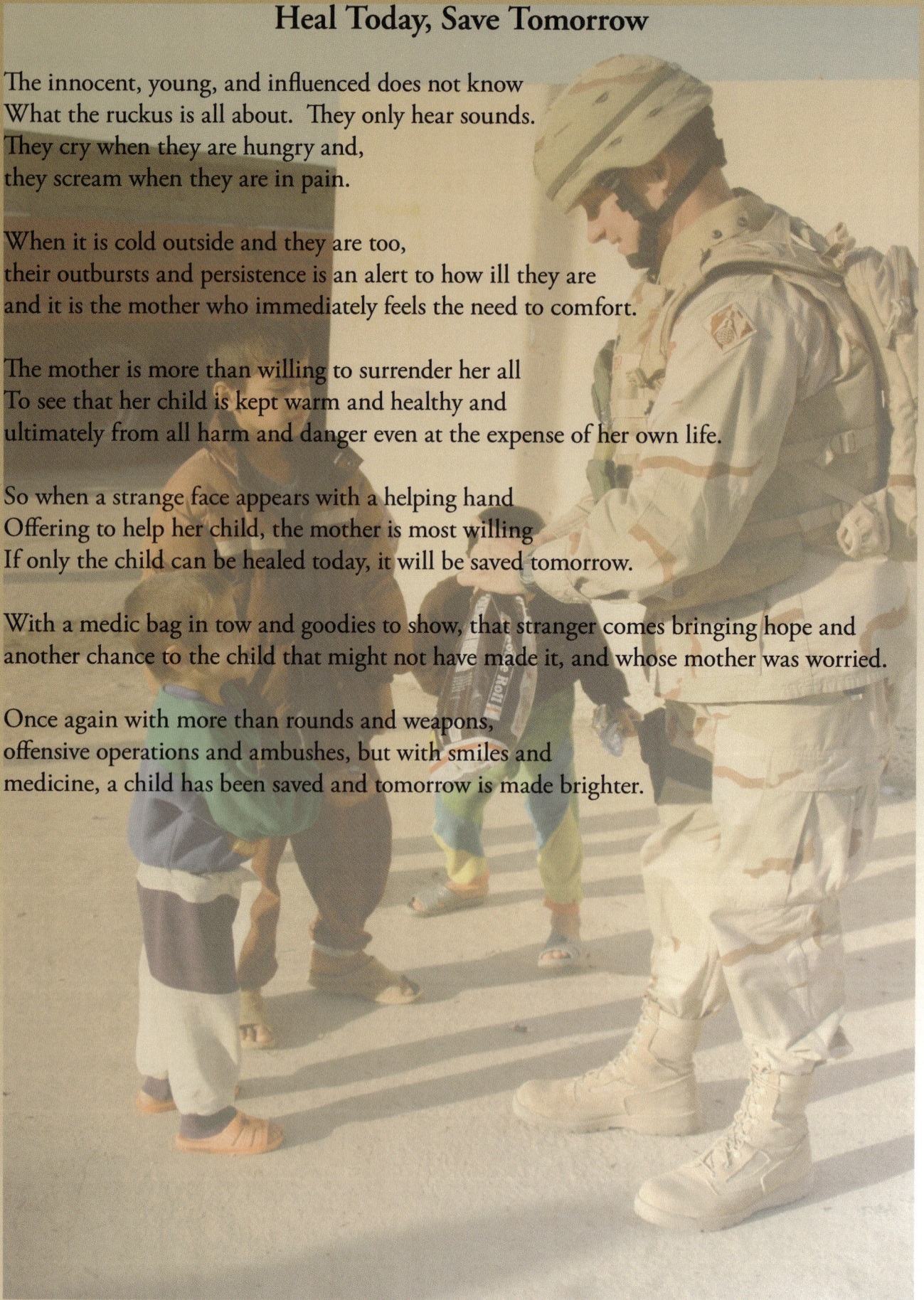

Hope in the Door

Standing in the doorway, the path is so unclear.
There is a keeper of the doorway and he has a key
There will be no more tyranny,
Nor any more threats.

The keeper of the doorway is wearing a protective vest.
Sometimes he is wearing a smile
Sometimes her face stern,
Just knowing that the door is covered
Takes care of many of the concerns.

Everyone gets to eat
No big I(s) and little you(s)
No haves and have nots
Everyone gets to have something.

Finally, a smile on that face that knew only frowns.
There is finally contentment where there was dissatisfaction.
Hope exists where dejection once thrived.

Hope is spelled a little different than what you knew.
Now it is spelled U-S-A-R-M-Y

So hold on tight and don't let go.
Hope is coming and there is more to go.
So when it is all said and done,
Hope will be there until the fear is gone.

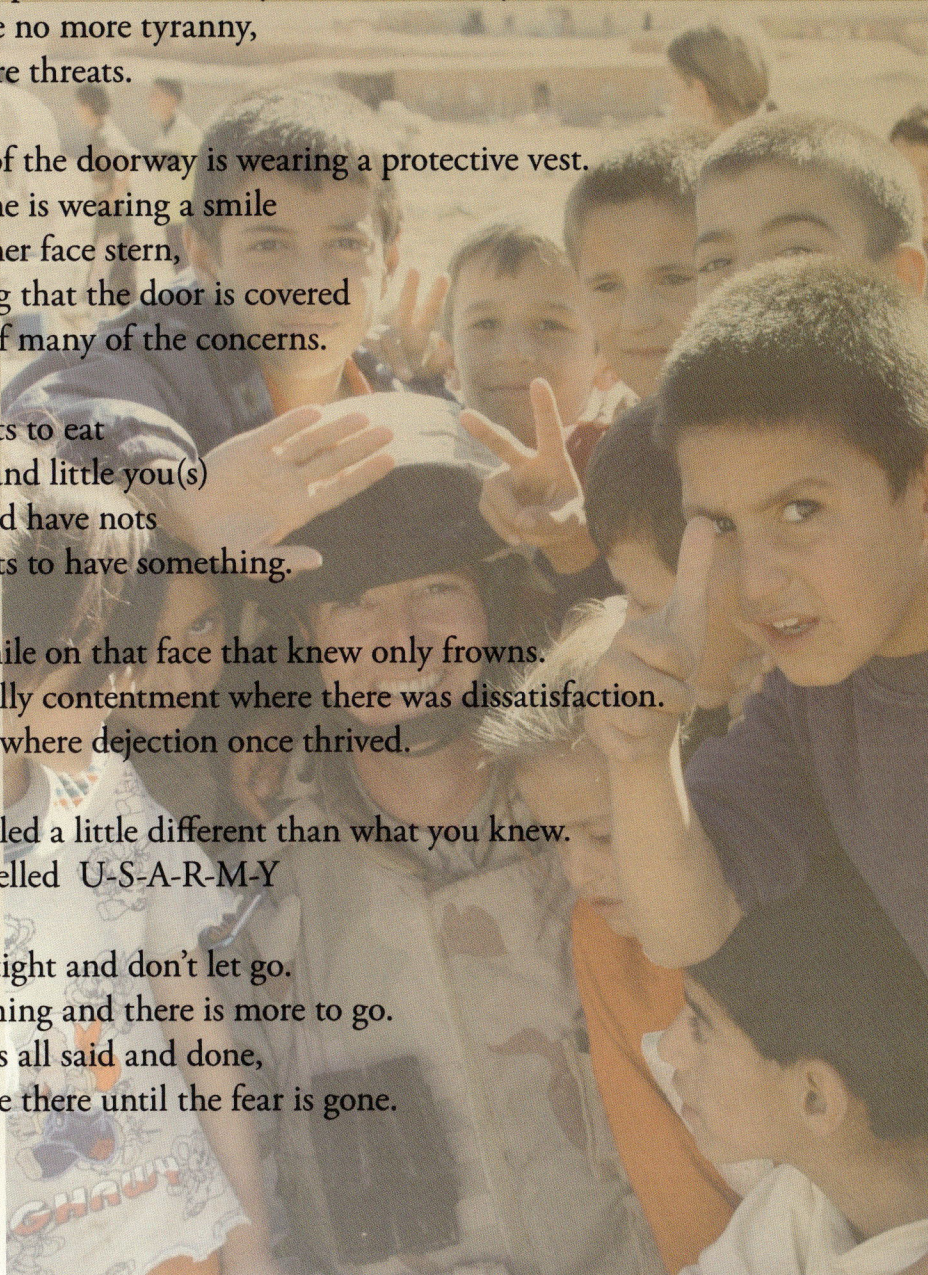

Hopeful Eyes in a Place of Despair

If the eyes be the entrance to the soul
Then what is the message that it sends?
As the door is left wide open for all to see.

For as much as it sees it still believes that there is a better day
Surrounded by chaos, mayhem and adversity
The soul holds out for more, this is only a snapshot in time.

Looking up, the eyes see what the future can hold
Inwardly, the soul yearns to become what it sees.
Someone who lives with freedom and liberty
Free to help others and lend a helping hand to lift someone's burden.

So in its limited ability to escape the surroundings,
The eyes cry out from the soul with a solemn voice
 "See my innocence in statue and time, but I have hope!"

Captured in place, captured in space and captured in time
Does not limit the future but only the present.
If these eyes can make it pass these times
Their hope for something better has a chance to be fulfilled.

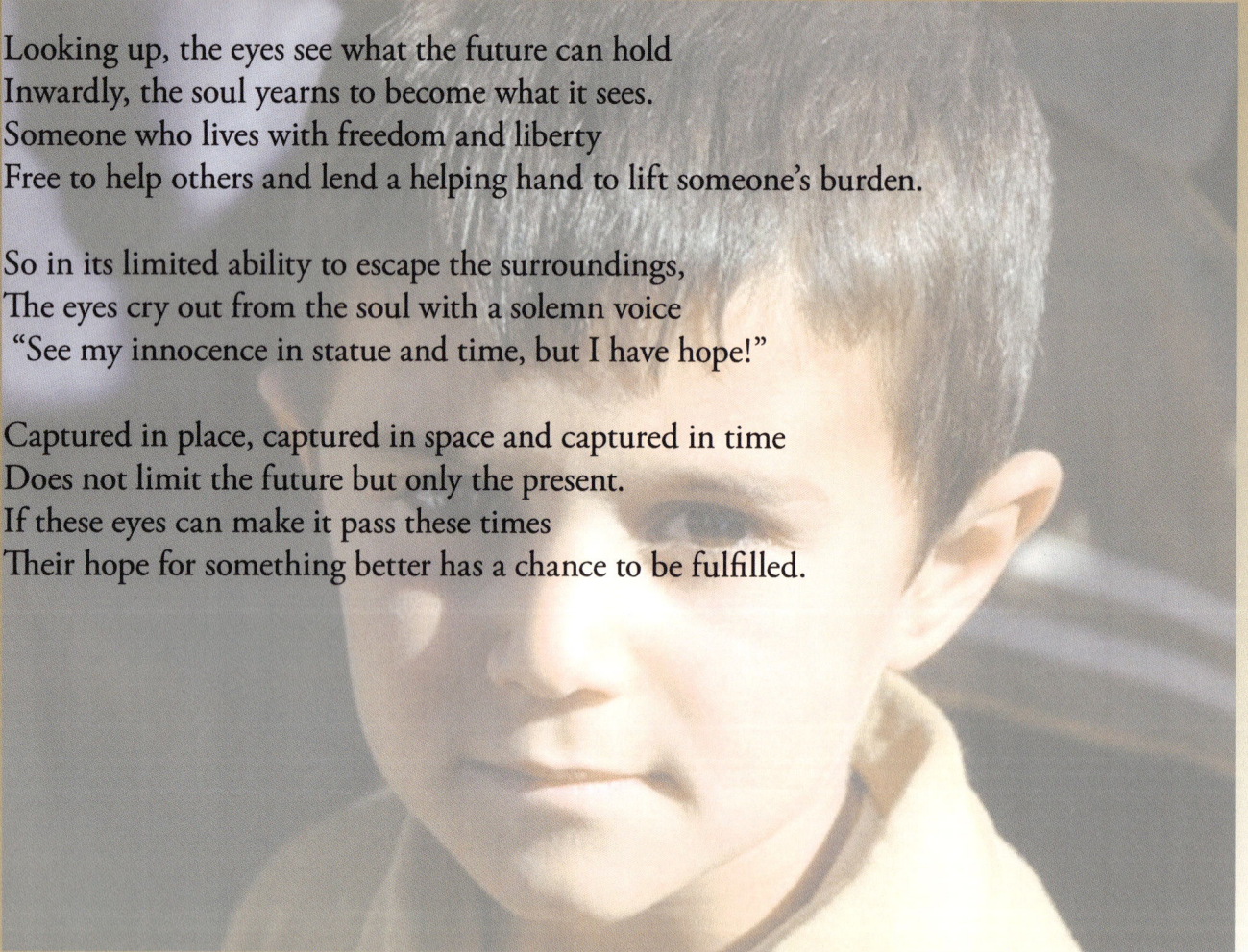

I Saw Mortality Today

How often in our childhood did it seem that we were invincible,
jumping off of rooftops and falling out of trees seemed to be such minor things.

Looking at thrillers and drama scenes on the latest weekend flicks,
seeing the performers long after they fall stand and later take their bow.

But on the field of battle when they fall they never stand again.
A fallen comrade becomes a memory. And we truly see their mortality.

We revel in their bravery,
Write books about their courage,
But we know their gift is a one-time offering.
It is the only thing they have, we have one life to live.

Not Like Heroes in Movies

Into the movies we charge to see the latest flicks.
Someone hanging from a building while kicking some butt
But its all theatrics and no one got hurt.

You see armies take out aliens, and one man takes out a gang.
But over in Iraq it is just not the same.

Bombs takes out convoys, RPGs take out trucks,
Insurgents kill innocent contractors,
And there are no heroes who knows every move of the
Enemy with a guarantee to take them out.

Only heroes in movies do the incredible feats.
The heroes in Iraq just keep fighting back.
No matter how tired they get,
They keep on taking it to them.

We wish our heroes were like those in the movies,
So when the day was over they would all get up,
dust themselves off, have a couple of cold ones,
and call it day, but not in Iraq.

In the Marketplace

How simplistic it seems that common folk would go down onto the street
And see side street vendors pedal their goods for daily needs
Choosing from the multiple options that lie beneath shoddy cloth sheets.

Simple it is not when you consider what all they had to go through
To bring their goods to market.
It was not enough they had to catch a ride, but furthermore, they had to avoid insurgent
gangs that would like to bring them harm.

Getting to market is no simple task. Rather it is a challenge.
Once getting there and setting up to offer their goods to the folks,
The whole ordeal, while watching who comes and goes is really not a joke.

They see suspicious cars and suspicious faces that pass like they don't belong,
Yet too conspicuously they give themselves away
Everyone knows they don't belong and they are way out of their way.

It's more than just a matter of watching the goods on the cart
It's a matter of watching the strangers move in cars
And making sure no one leaves one unattended with a ticker just inside.

So in the marketplace where there are many faces and so many vendors
There is more for sale than produce,
What you might find you may wish you had rather left behind while visiting in the market.

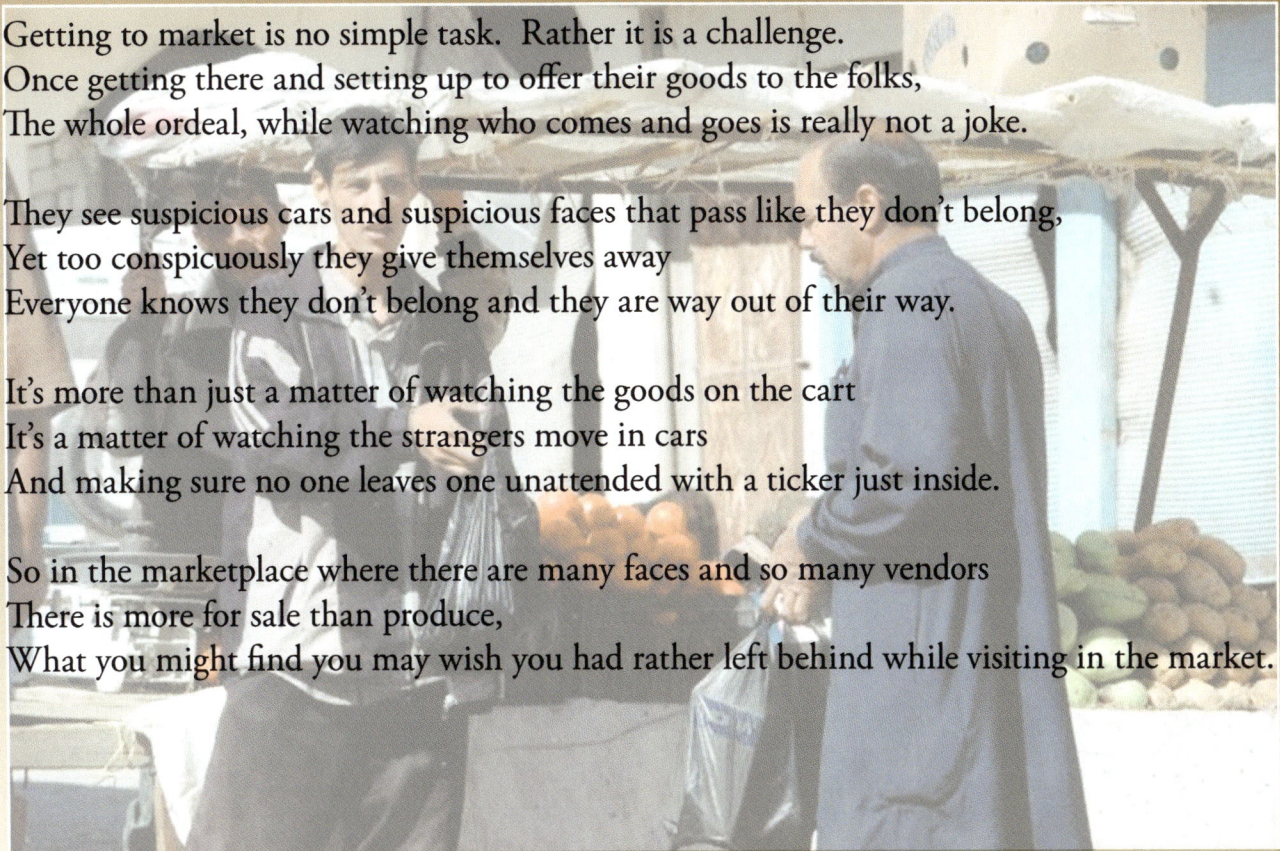

In the Shadows, But Out Front

Back in the shadows and away from the crowd
A humble figure squats down with a smile fixed upon her face
She is looking upon her labor, steps forward, and extends a greeting.

Each child is like a branch on a tree attached to the trunk.
The branches stand beyond reach, the trunk yet attached.
They represent how the branches shall see what the trunk never will.

The branches shall reach over the fence and see into other gardens
Their eyes shall behold the freedoms that from which they came could not imagine
Their strength will be steadfast, their hope will be sustained, and their visions realized.

In the shadows, an image of a strong trunk overlooks her branches of her tree.
Her masculine branches, she lets them venture farther from her reach, yet she sees them.
Her feminine branches, she draws them near to her, not to limit their reach, but to protect their progress.

The latter shall be greater than the former.
Just as the branches shall go where the trunk never could
The branches shall reach out front and the trunk will keep to the shadows.

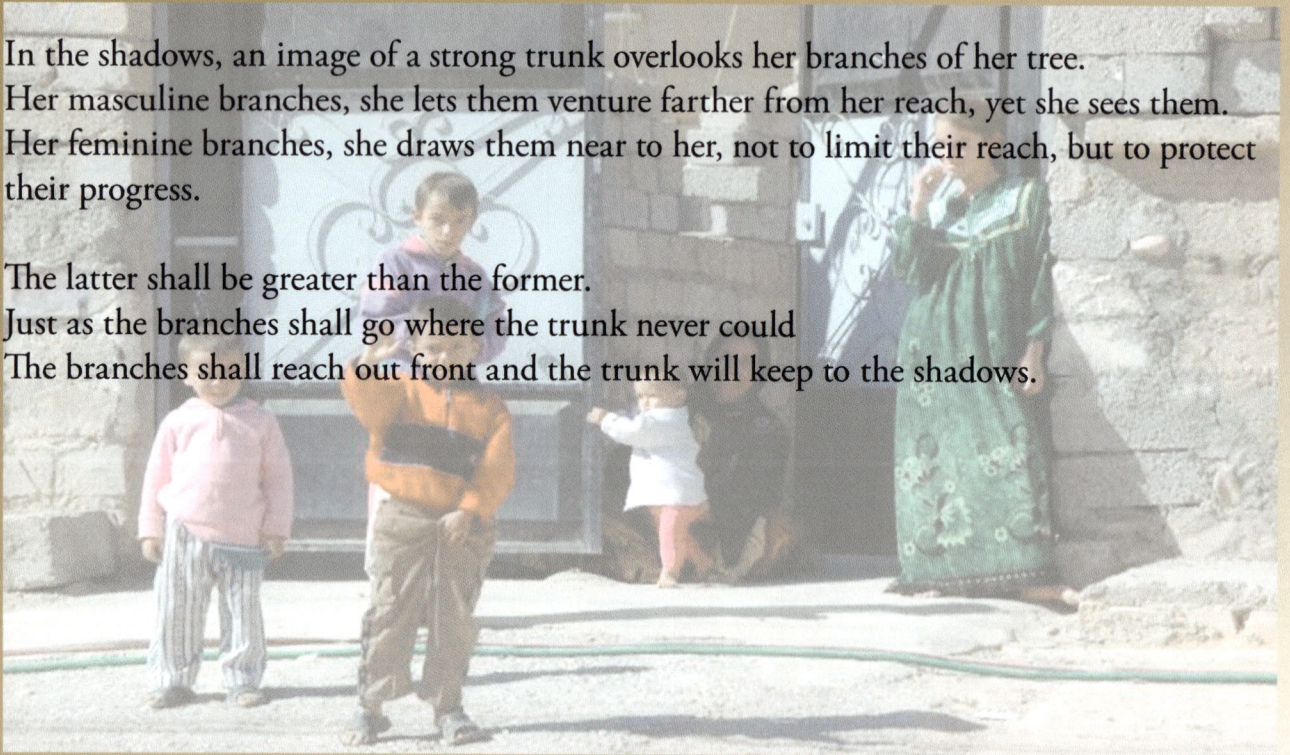

Innocence and the Keepers

Innocence in the middle of the streets
With smiles across their faces
Waving ever so jovially with desolation on either side.

Behind them lies a dark corridor
Dim lit where they wish not to go
But in the presence of the keepers
Their fear is put to rest.

Congregated together, youngest to oldest
The innocent looks with hope.
There is far less concern on the streets
than in some ally where insurgents they could meet.

The streets are dangerous and filled with harm,
But dark alleys are not a charm.
Given a choice, they would rather be with the
Peacekeepers because they know what they do are good.
They help the poor, feed the hungry and make all the bad go away.

Innocence and the peacekeepers.
Peace is all the innocent want.

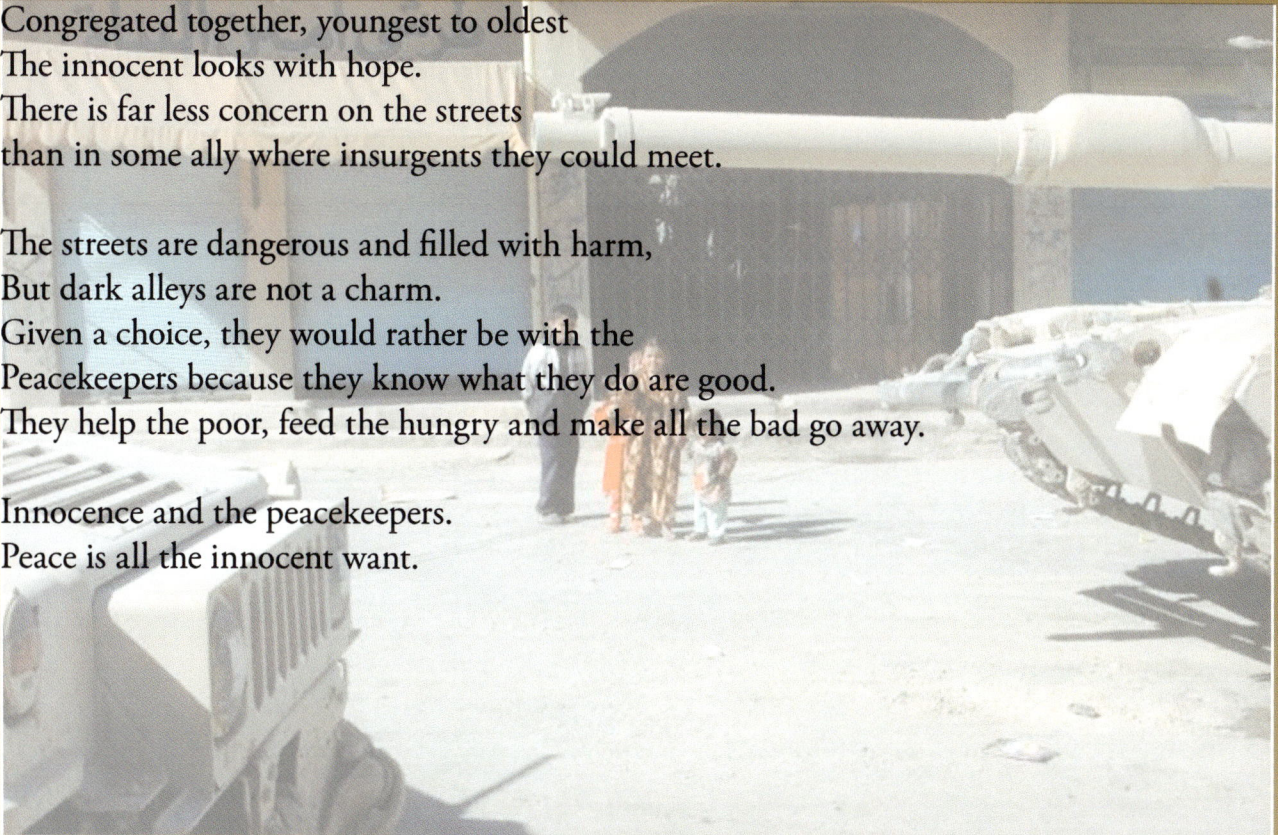

Joint Forces, Joint Success

A harden soldier trained to lead
He has learned the old principle of air, land and sea.
But he has also learned new principles
And he now teaches how to win a battle this way.

He brings all his experiences from leading small groups,
Teaching his platoon how to move and shoot.
He advanced these skills to a point where he can teach
Now he is trainer of an Iraq Army team.

He will teach the Iraqi Army how to fight and move
How to attack and secure a position
So the enemy will not get out of a noose.

They will learn how to fight like Rangers fight
How to move into place, setup an ambush
And all this at night.

They will learn how to travel in convoys
So their men will not get blown up.
They will perfect the skill of how to button up.

We have joined forces so that we both will win
Because the coalition force can't win unless the Iraqi join in.
So join forces to have joint success.
If we are ever going to leave, this choice is the best.

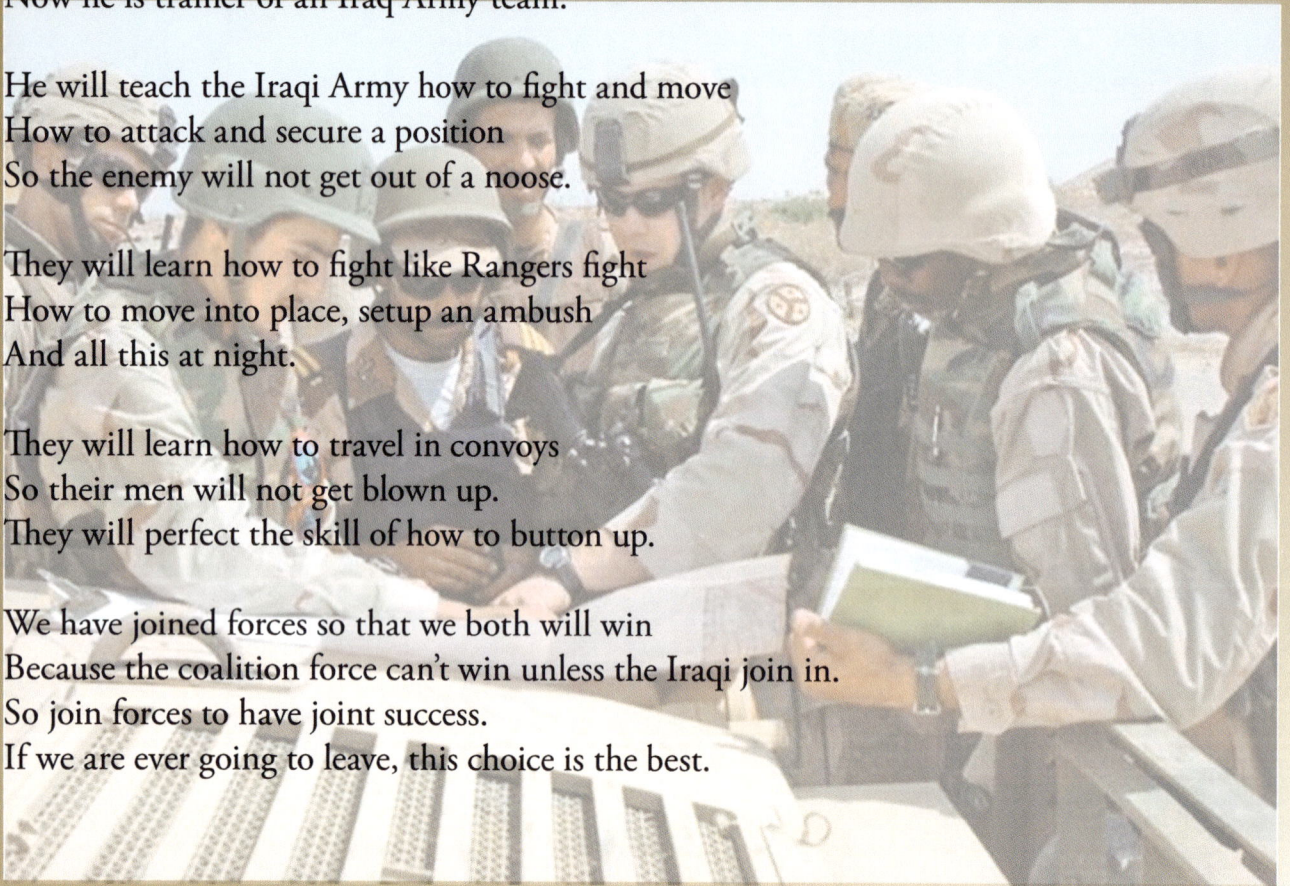

Leaders Cry Too

When you see leaders standing tall
Espousing great ideas and plans for soldiers to accomplish
And citing great visions as to just how they see a mission end
They are at their greatest.

These leaders will lead soldiers through hell's gates
And step in front of Satan himself and demand his surrender
And return all that he has stolen from innocent people.

But out of the presence of all the faces of the crowd
in the dark quarters when that leader finally calls it a day,
second thoughts cross their minds.
Alternate options and other choices that could have been taken are pondered.

Every face of fallen soldiers under their command is replayed in their mind, the time and
place of his demise. At that very moment, memorializing that soldier is an infamous
moment.

So when a leader stands aside seeing one more valiant warrior
memorialized, and looking upon his deeds and those that will
remember this warrior forever, and you see that leader wipe their
eyes, know that in spite of what you have seen, they add one more face to their dream filled
night.

Lean On Me, Brother!

They are the ground ponders, the cannon cockers and the loggies.
They are the transporters, the scouts and the mud puppies out in
the cities, shaking the bush, cordoning off areas to secure the block.

But on every mission, down every road, on every convoy, hearts
are racing at a hundred miles per hour. Eyes are fixed for the smallest thing out of place,
while ears are perched to pick up the slightest change in pitch or sound.

In a split second, taking rounds seemingly from everywhere,
Seeing vehicles disintegrate before their eyes,
Hearing commands being called for cover or return fire
Brothers at arms see their brothers fall in the crossfire wounded.

Pent down by overwhelming danger, "Horsemen and Ghost Riders" see their best friends'
lives ebb and flow beyond their reach. Too far to reach them, too far gone to save them
Brothers at arms are forced to part ways one more time.

Another friend is gone from the crew. Another team member will not answer to their
name, and another name will be added to the scroll. But most of all, another family
member from the brotherhood is missing.

Everyone is shaken; the most is upon the closest of family members, but it becomes the
duty of older brothers to hold the younger ones. When the younger brothers break down in
tears remembering the good times, it is the older ones who shift a shoulder, grab them near,
giving them comfort with words of hope in their ear.

It's all good brothers. We share the pain.

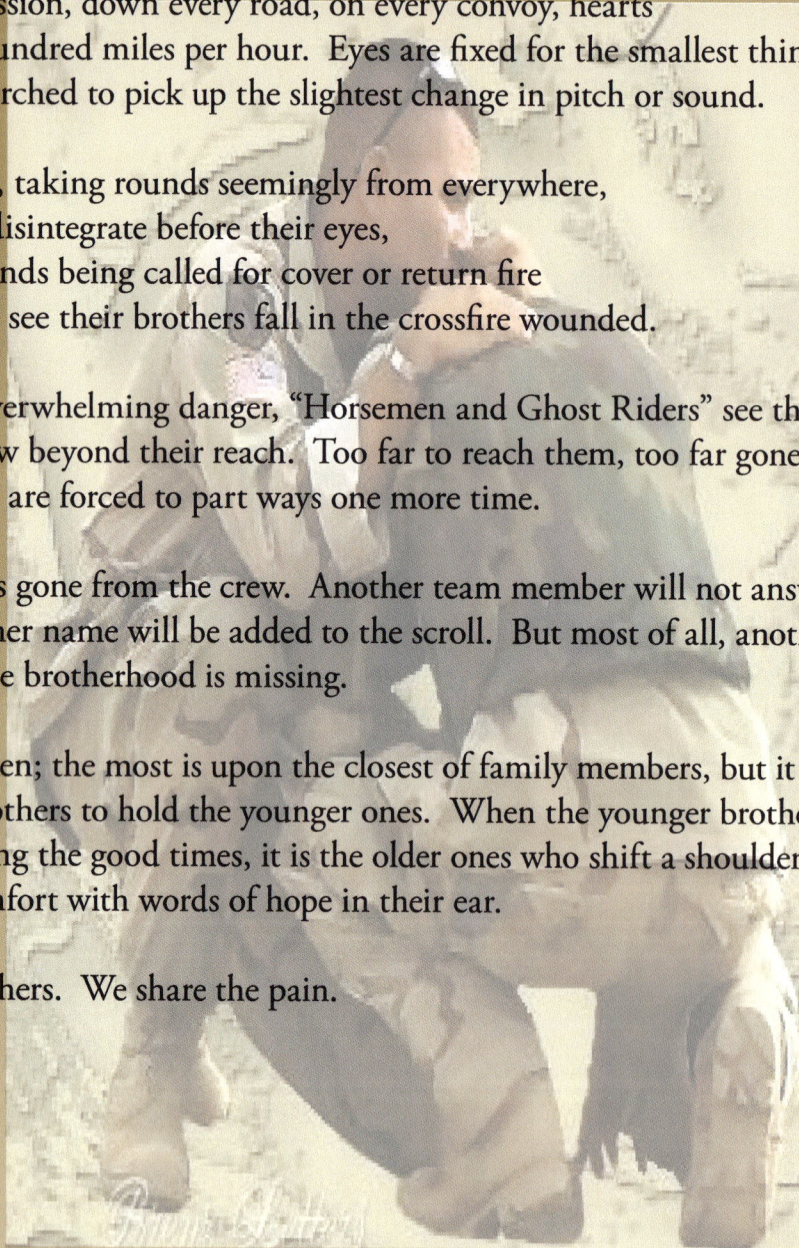

Life Preservers

Through the toil of racking their minds, they persist to
learn the anatomy of humankind. The more that is known,
the better they are tending to ailments that leave others in awe.

Hours and hours behind a book, they must learn the fibula and all the vessels through
which blood runs, and what in the body causes negative reaction to the sun.

Caduceus is their symbol and medicine their professional
calling. They know no rest. With every code blue, they are
taking a test. The results of the test is life or death, therefore, their aim is to do their best.

With every passing day, a new discovery is made to evade some sickness, or treat it at least.
A day is not done until they have defeated this beast, death.

In the ICU, the OR, the trauma center or wherever it may be, these professionals stand
ready to face the grim features of death head on, and defeat it if they can. Maybe, just to
relieve the pain from an agonizing woman or man.

As their symbol connotes that in the face of death and danger they are the avenging angels
with wings, there to save the day, to extend life one hour, one day, one week, one month or
even several decades.

Fear not, for those that don the wings on a staff encircled by serpents come to revive, give
life, and right the wrongs that exist in the bodies of mankind.
They are the willing made able to attend to the creation of the creator, for they are the
Enhancers of life.

So for all the long hours they stand awake working to improve someone's life,
It must be understood that they are the gifts of angels sent down to attend to the welfare of
men.
Those who serve continue to preserve life and extend life so others may live long lives.
For the lives that are saved, someone is smiling instead of crying. Therefore, to those who
such symbols adorn their lapels, carry on so others may live and live long.

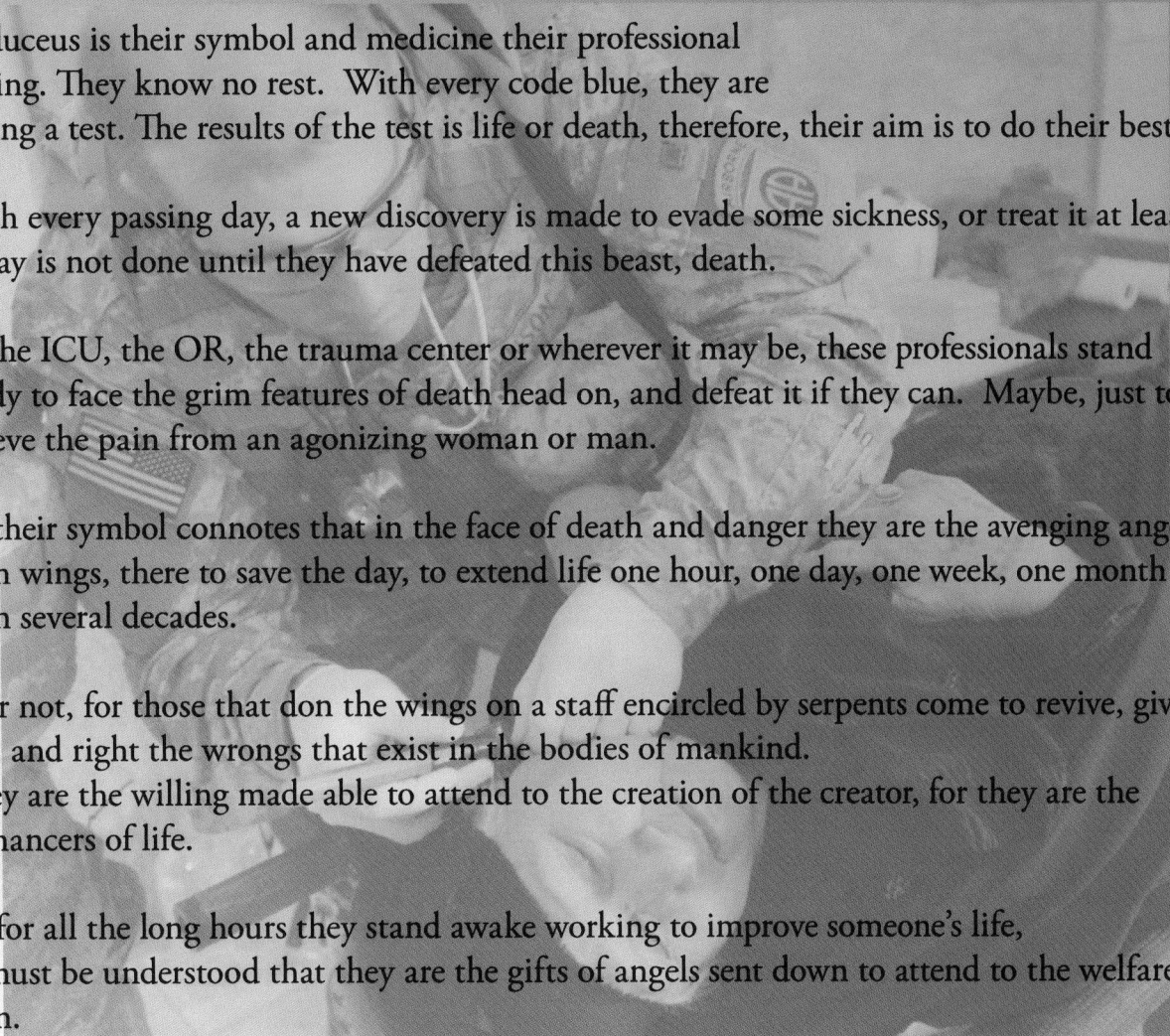

Little Girl, Future Hope

She is angelic in her appearance.
You would think she is a doll, not at all real,
Looking for a pair of shoes to put on her heels.

What a backdrop the surrounding countryside cast
Wondering villagers seeing to their tasks.
Adorable children at play in the valley completely unaware of the violence around them.

Unbeknownst to the children that is cheerfully at play
There is a storm brewing and it is heading their way.
If only their innocence can be shielded, or their minds kept from corruption.

Let the little girl grow up with hope instead of dread.
Let her walk about with an uncovered head.
Let her not hide her smile but expose it in full.
Let her future be bright not covered under clay.

May her gait be filled with pride not hampered by fear.
May her heart be lifted with hope, not burdened by tyranny.
May her dreams be fulfilled, and her fantasies to be seen.

Her future is riding on our backs.
Her dreams are filtered by Americans presence.
Visitors who see beyond her moment generate her smile.

Little girl of golden curls
On a stage with a backdrop on the side of a hill,
Hope for your future, while we deliver you your dreams.

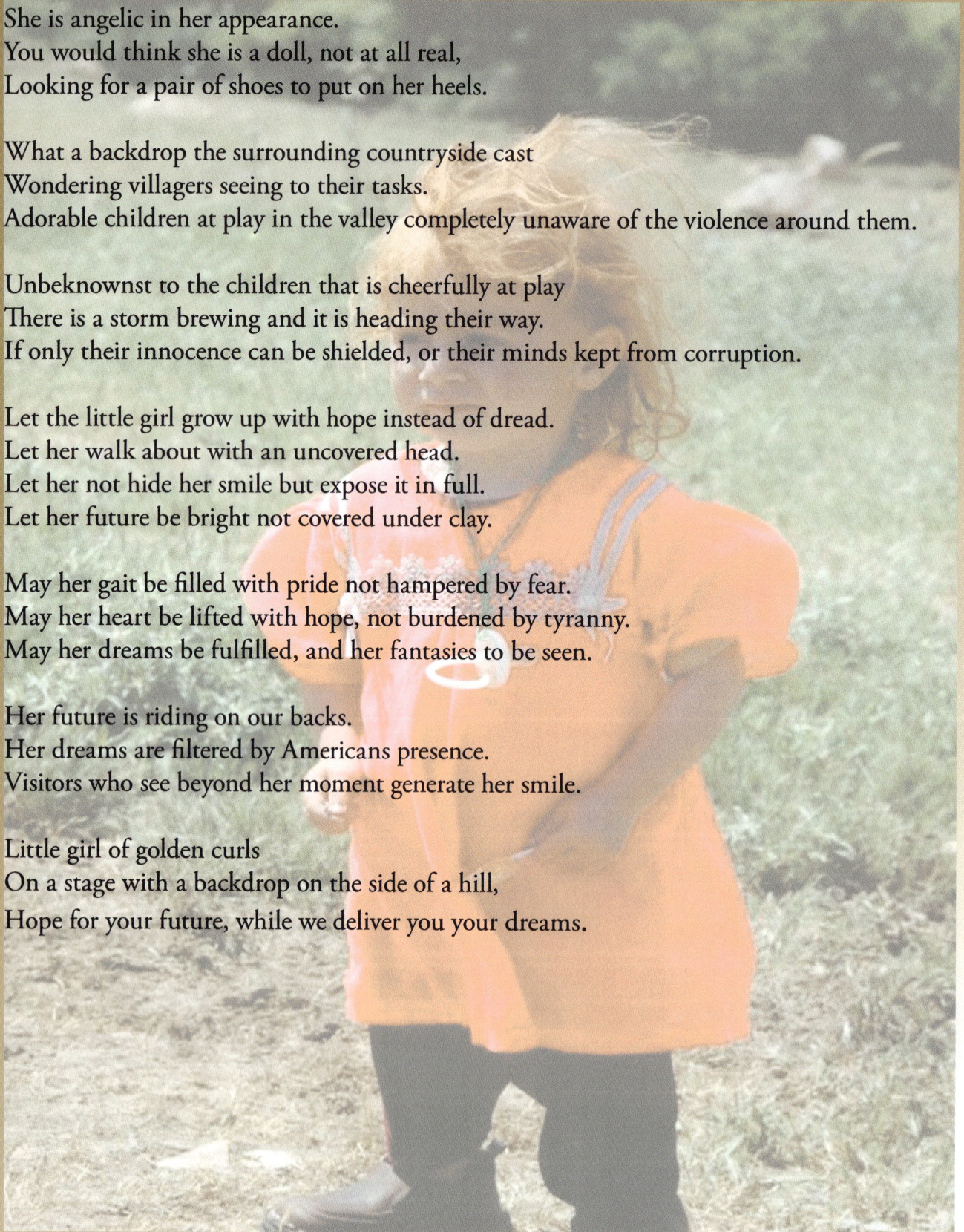

Man's Best Friend

They may be hairy all over and walk on four legs
Beg for scraps then stand on their hind legs
But they're more than just animals, they are soldiers too.

They go on patrols sniffing things out front
Making sure no mines are set
that might take off a soldier's foot.

They check buildings for explosives
to make sure they are all clear.
They are trained to pick up that smell and they have a good ear.

If you are looking for the enemy
down some long alleyway,
There is no better soldier to have going your way.

They don't wear IBA to protect them like we do
But they have a mission that no one else can do
And that is to hunt it down and find it and they do.

So they are more than just hounds or shepards
But they are watchmen and point men.
They are not just dogs, but friends.
We're thankful for them for they save our skin.

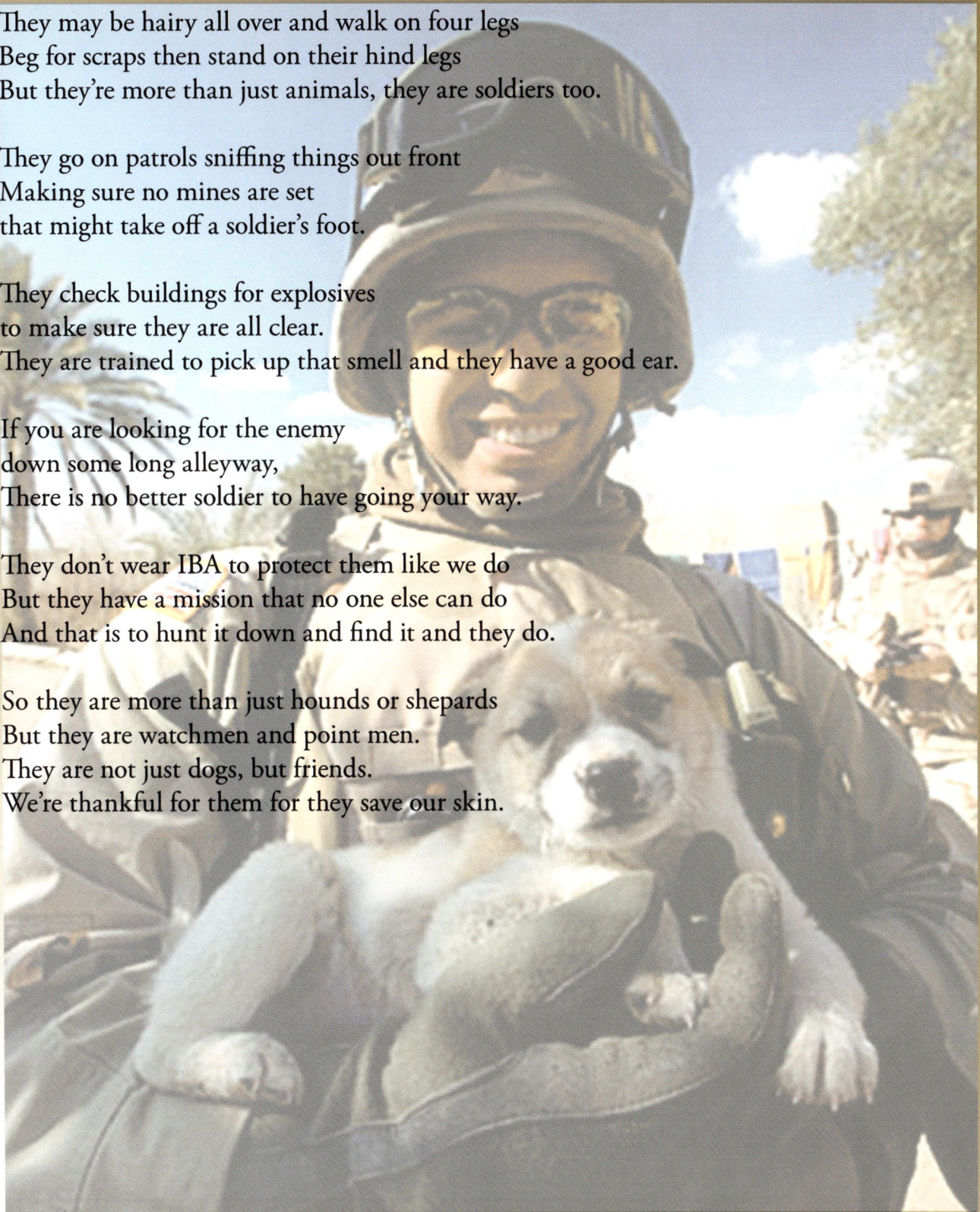

Marching to the Cadence

In this age of Global War on Terrorism, soldiers who are men and women daily pack their bags, put their affairs in order, say goodbye to their families and love ones, salute the flag and head off to some foreign country for battle. They are required to exercise everything that they have learned through their military career to the test. The one thing that they will remember the most from all their training is working together. It all began when they first came into the military and they were called to fall into formation. Once they had fell into formation, they were marched to the destination hearing a rhythmic lyric they would come to know as cadence. This cadence, which taught them how to be in unison as a unit, also taught them to be alert of their surroundings, and how to work as a team. As each individual walks, marches, skips, it doesn't matter; they were always unconsciously conscious that they were in sync with each other. So as they deploy to some distant shore, they are about holding on to the pride of the organization, keeping in step with the unit, but most of all keeping up with a buddy.

Every soldier is dedicated to the armed forces that they joined whether it be Army, Marine, Navy or Air Force, it doesn't matter. This began when they first raised their hand, signed on the dotted line and took the oath to serve. They were committed to that service. Being committed to that service says that they took on a certain frame of mind associated with that service simply by association if nothing more. Being in the Army as infantry, you don't live there unless you know what "Hoooaah" means. In the Marines, you have to know what it is to be ""Semper Fi". Each of the services has their key jargons and code words that solely identify them from the others. But even more, within each of the forces there are sub-communities that exist. They range anywhere from the Rangers to Recon to SEALS. But in between all of these are the regular forces that make up the body that keep these special pieces rolling like engineers, admin, logistics and transportation. Each one is dependent upon the other, synchronizing each task to meet the others' needs to ensure the mission is done on time, to specification and to standard.

Each discipline works by the same rules as the others. Each area has principles that is unique to them, and they will work within those principles to make sure they and other team members are successful because infantryman cannot fight without the bullets from logistics, and logistics cannot get the bullets unless transportation delivers, and transportation can't deliver unless ordinance have the caliber on hand. Everyone marches in cadence, so the organization is always on beat. They even break themselves down into battle operating systems, BOSes. They are battle operating systems that define how each specialty support the other. What makes them special? What do they bring to the fight? What is their worth in the large frame of things? Commitment to the organization sets the stage so everyone in each armed force operates by a certain principle within that organization.

Each soldier, marine, sailor and airman has committed themselves to their organization. They know their service songs, they know their service's history, they know their service's greatest heroes and icons; they are committed to their armed service.

But the commitment does not end at the organization, it only begins there. Within each armed service there are those units that historically standout above the rest. They have a legacy that is colorful and distinguished. It is not enough that you know the organization's song, but you must know the unit's history. It is a matter of knowing where they have been, knowing all of their successes as well as their failures that makes them the units they have become. The leaders of these units study their predecessors, learning from their actions. From this knowledge, these units obtain strength and courage to forge a way into the future.

New recruits are drilled to know every battle drill to perfection. Junior leaders are trained to exhaustion how to be the best leaders they can be, and what it takes to bring every solider home in the unit, the company, or the squad size element that they are assigned to. Endlessly the cycle is repeated; the old teach the young who becomes old, who again teaches a younger one so that the ideals of the former leaders are continuously passed on. Each soldier proudly adorns each unit's crest signifying dedication and commitment. They cry out with the unit's motto and when meeting one another will again sound off with a chosen out cry.

So when they go into battle, soldiers hold fast to their training, every drill that was rehearsed until exhausted, and the very spirit of the unit. They hoist their unit symbol above where they live as if to say, "Yeah, this is where we are and if you want some of us just dare cross that line and you are going to get a piece what you see". Their scores are not so much compared to fellow soldiers but to their unit's legacies such as "we stand alone" or "cold steel".

But more than anything else, these soldiers are bound to their buddies. It is their buddies that they have history with. The one friend that was there when another ran out of money and a friend gave him just enough to hold him over. Then it was the one pal that helped her buddy when she really needed a hand and her best friend was there for her. So when units deploys, soldiers go prepared so they will not let their buddies down.

Each of them, at some obscure time, shares a secret with that special friend of "if something happens, do this". And being the friend that the other is, they will ensure nothing will happen, but if it does, they will make sure their friends' wishes are met. So each service member, while committed to country and unit, they will fight and die for their fellow service members who they see everyday. Their commitment is not delineated by ethnicity, origin, race or creed, but by their standing there in the foxhole or turret with their comrades.

For as much as each of the services has their mottos from "This We Will Defend" to "Simper Fidelis", those quotes translated between service members is "I am with you in the fight" and "Simply whatever the Cost", there is no turning back. Every soldier on the field fights for the other, never wanting to let their peers or friends down. Yes, they know the lineage of the unit and how it fought in previous conflicts, but the defining factor is that moment where they are, what they are going through, and most of all, that is my buddy. The commitment is overwhelming; It forces those in pain and fear to go through it in spite of it. So you see, while every soldier is deployed to support the commands of those over him or her, and to uphold the constitution, there is more to the story. They are fighting not only for the guy or girl that is their terrain coordinator, TC, or their assistant gunner who is carrying more ammo, but also for their squad that is pinned down in the fight. They are fighting for one another, nothing less. Yes, they will salute the flag and cry "hoooaah!" They will lift the flag high as they run with it in formations. They will stand when they hear the national anthem played. Furthermore, they will always stand up proud, proudly showing that they are Americans. But when the tracers start to fly and 40mm start to impact, it's about who is to their left and right. They are not just fighting for what is back home, but they are willing to sacrifice for their fellow man. Each live by a time honored adage, "What greater sacrifice than a man who would lay down his life for a friend." So when one of their numbers has fallen, you will always see the grief because another friend has given his greatest sacrifice and those left behind are honored to have been called friends.

In the Face of Losses, Spirits Renewed

How does one continue when they see their loved ones'
life stolen from them, not by old age or a biological discease,
but by violence at the hand of someone for whom no wrong was done.

Oh how the soul wails at the loss.
The chest builds to a bellow and flows outwardly.
Memories like short mpeg replays in the mind recalling great events.
The moment is saturated with remorse and grief for a loss that can't be undone.

How many lives are affected by this loss; it's truly impossible to tell.
It is truly a chain-link affect, with one link cut from the chain.
How many other links will lose their anchor?

For as much as the moment pains, there is invigoration.
There are the images of great fathers and great mothers.
There are the memories of great family times together.
Above all, there is the heart-felt knowledge of being loved and loving back.

From this moment onward, yes there are those that will not be here
No smiles to see, no hands to hold, and no gradual images of getting older. No more inside
jokes, but all is not lost.

In the face of the moment, there are the great times of togetherness.
Those times that marked a turning point forever.
Those moments that lives like yesterday; they are so fresh.
By this, the spirit is renewed, the heart is strengthened, and there is pride that you knew
them and they are a part of you.

Memorial Moments

Water wells up from the depth of the soul
The heart is heavy laden and it can no longer stand bold
Too many thoughts rips at the mind
Remembering a fellow soldier now left behind.

No more challenges to see who is the best
No more chants to get that weight off their chest
No more pictures with friends just before a mission
All that's left are memories.

A room full of buddies
Old friends and leaders alike
Looking upon a pair of boots, a helmet, and a rifle with a bayonet
All the things a soldier carries with their Kevlar vest.

Worse of all is the formation
Called to attention
When the roll is called the soldier name is never answered.

That's another warrior gone down doing their best
It's another friend that we will always carry in our chest.
Taps will never be just another tune in the middle of the night
This moment will last forever long after the tears are dry.

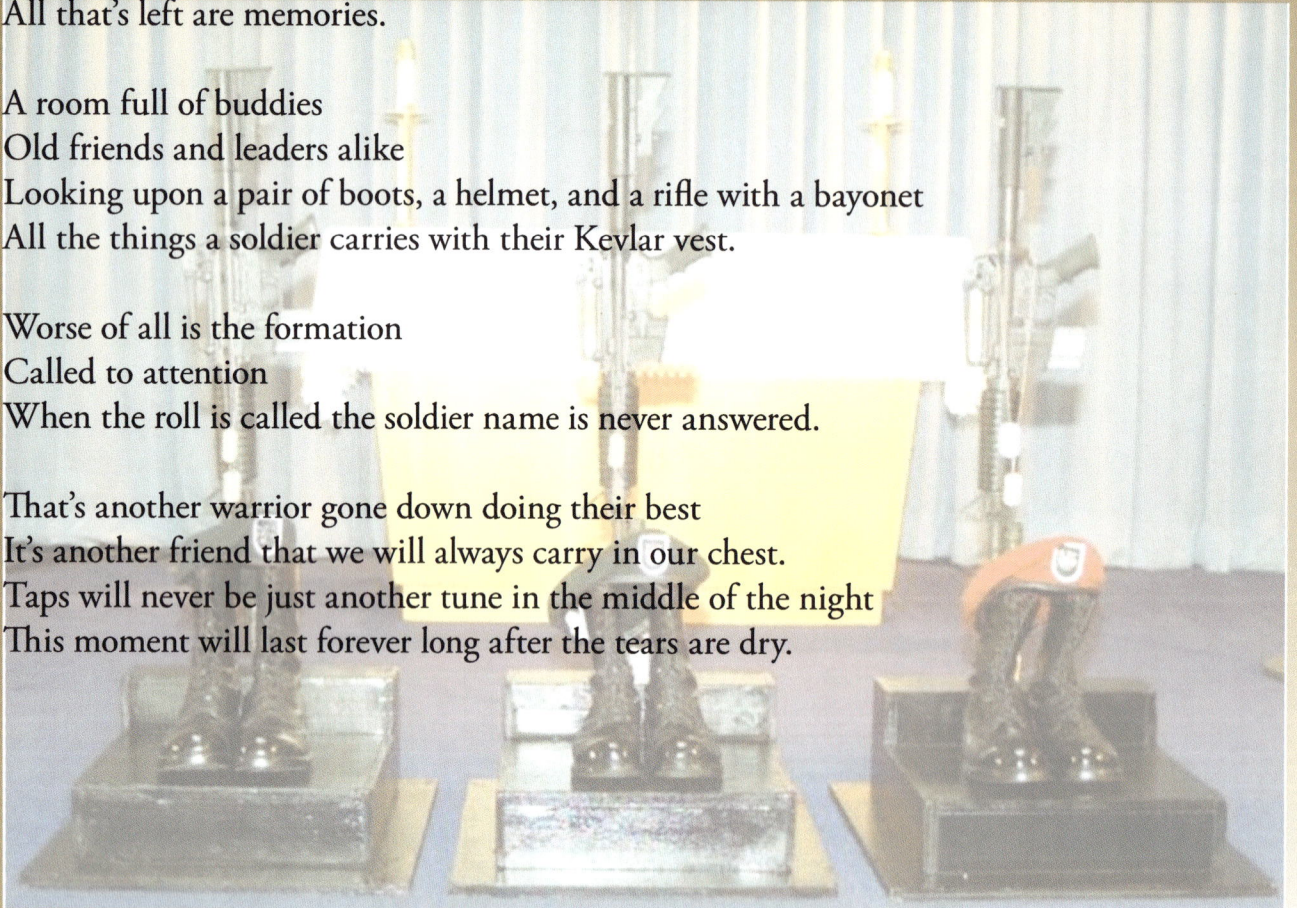

Medals from Iraq

Since the very first day that soldiers hit the ground
Everyone have been talking about the combat medals
The infantry medal, the combat medal, the expeditionary medal.

Everyone wants that medal
So they can wear it across their chest
Telling a story of sacrifice and their bravery
And how each one of them did their best.

You get a Silver Star for valor
If you fought the enemy under fire
You didn't retreat, you stood your ground
and really lay on the heat.

You get a Bronze Star with v devise
If you fought but not as great
As the Silver Star wearer and when they
Stood up to the enemy face to face.

And you get a Distinguish Service Medal
If you did darn well and contributed to the mission at hand
You are recognized and hands are shook and you are the one with the plan.

But then you have the medals that no one wants at all
They are the prosthetic hands, the prosthetic arms, the prosthetic legs and feet
These are the medals that many soldiers wear for valor and gallantry in war.

Others can remove their medals and go about their merry way
But the wearers of those prosthetic medals
Must wear their medal always.

We salute those Silver Stars, Bronze Stars and all
But most of all, we salute our prosthetic medal wearers
Because they gave their all.

Mortality in Battle

How often in our childhood did it seem that we were invincible?
Jumping off of rooftops and falling out of trees seemed to be such minor things.
Looking at thrillers and drama scenes on the latest weekend flicks
Seeing the performers long after they fell, later stand and take their bow.

But on the field of battle when they fall they never stand again
If one of the soldiers is in an explosion, they are not seen in another scene.
They are only mourned; everyone knows that they are not coming back on stage.

How quickly is a close comrade or buddy taken?
When they were just there yesterday, tomorrow they are gone.
Could it be that they are gone or have they only rotated out?

With every increase in the number count, there is one less of us
One less buddy, one less pal, one less confidant, one less soldier
A fallen comrade.

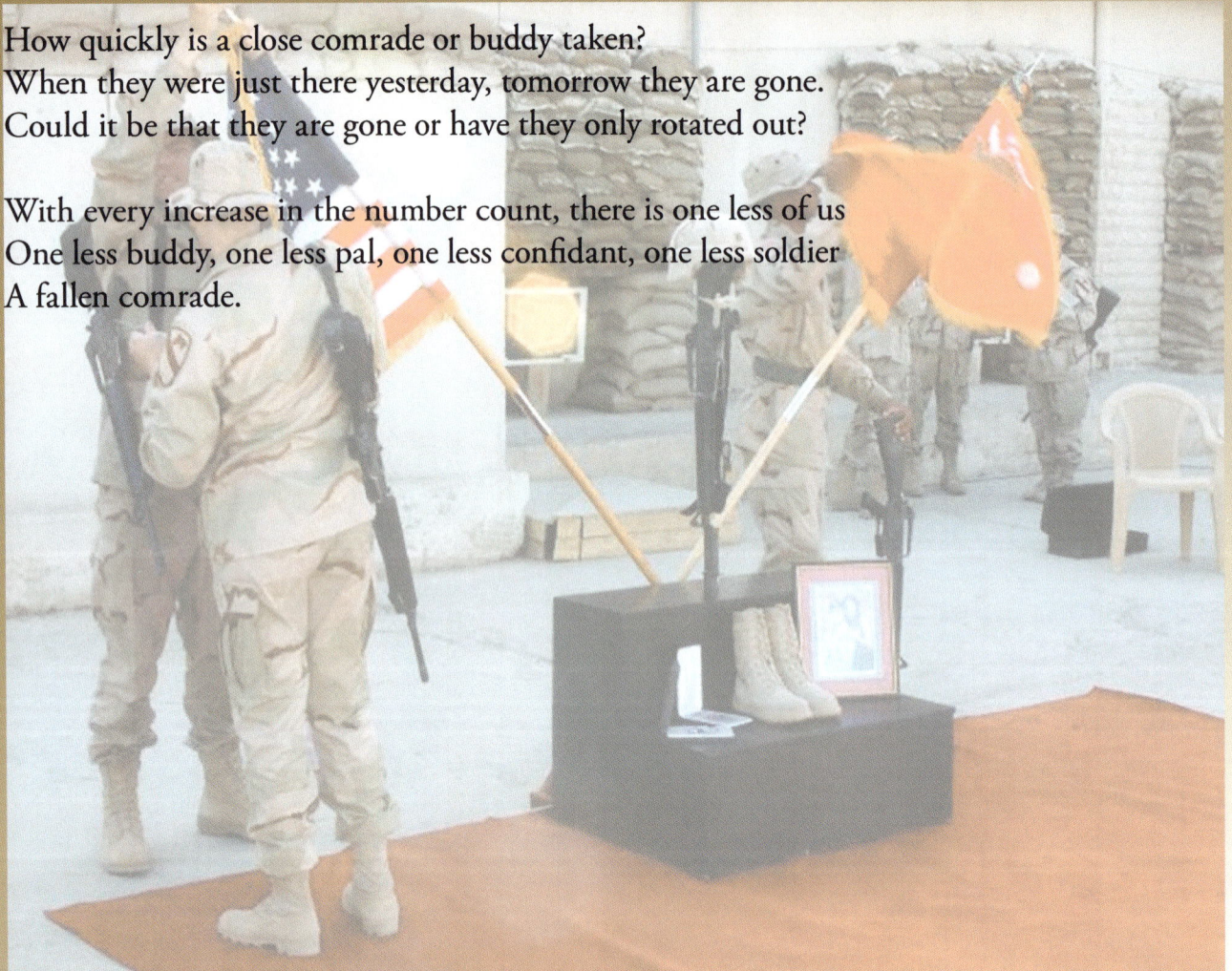

My Country Tis of Thee

What is my country really to me?
It's more than the red, white and blue
Although those colors linger in my mind.

It's more than "these solemn rights we hold true"
Although these words constitute our inalienable rights
We are all equal, divided not by gender, race, religion or origin.

My country to me is my fellow soldier,
Not for the color I see
But for the soldier I am, for they are like me.

In the eyes of my country, I see its' greatest.
I see its' diversity of many hues and shades.
It is many nationalities and many beliefs.

My country to me is country-western, rock, and jazz
It is hip-hop, blues and classical.
It's the soul of every American.

My country is the platoon on patrol,
With women and men.
They are African American, Asian American,
Hispanic, and of Hebrew descent—yet all are American

I don't know them by their heritage
Rather I know them by their commitment, their allegiance.

My country to me is not the small town I came from,
but the great nation that surrounds me.
My country is my fellow soldier, my country tis of thee.

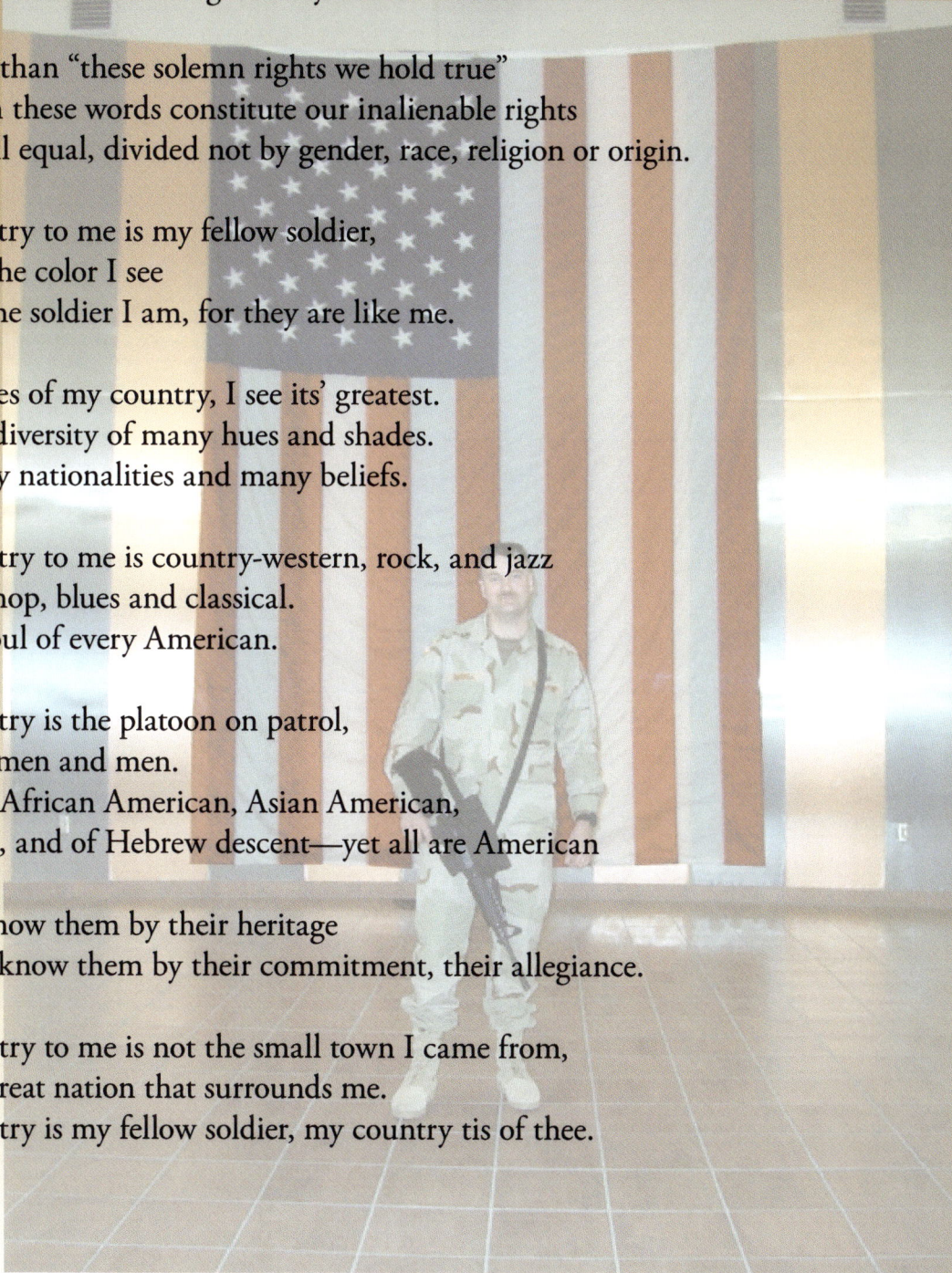

Deeds; Where Words Won't Do

What a day when right before your eyes all you see is a fireball and debris and scrap metal is flying everywhere.

What was once your best friend's vehicle in front is now only a pile of rubble burning fiberglass with a stench.

With a burst windshield, a half blown hood, everything is in a haze as you see fellow soldiers scramble about trying to secure your position from small arms fire.

The best that can be mustered, I'm not dead. With a bloody face, ballistic shades peppered with shrapnel, words evade the moment.

All that is known is not this one, not this time and not today but words can't describe it; just look at the image and it will speak.

My Soldier Made It Back To Me

For twelve long months, minus two weeks, her soldier has been away.
She had to be mother, father, and the everything in her house, but
that faithful day has arrived.

She got up early and did her hair, put on her face with some tender loving care.
Looking in the back of the closet she got her dress, put it on, she
was at her best.

Three nights before, she'd talked to her soldier.
They talked about the kids, how things were at home, and how they loved each other.
All the other little stuff that husband and wife talk about.

He got a little frisky while talking in a whispering tone.
She behaved like a schoolgirl, blushing and carrying on.

He told her in hours how long he had left.
She started counting the minutes.
She could not believe it herself.

All the kids were nicely dressed.
Can't wait for their dad to come home.
The smallest son kept calling his name and
The daughter kept looking to see if he had come.

When he stepped in the auditorium
Where all the family members were standing
He heard his name yelled and his heart went racing.

Looking at this family, from his wife to his kids
He knew that he was blessed
As he hugged his wife and children,
He knew he could finally rest.

No Rest For The Weary

Everyone wants peace they say and will do whatever it takes.
So how far will they go to get it?
Will they give up comfort and all those niceties?
For run down pieced together living conditions

Peace does not come without its cost.
It is not easily earned.
And it is not comfortable while being obtained.

City policemen huddle in makeshift rooms,
windows covered by cardboard as renovations
take place around them, a promise of a better day.

To serve and protect is their aim
So they surrender their ideas of what could be nice.
Surrounding them in streets are those that are fatigued and shattered.
They are the ones that truly matter.

So for the sake of the city's citizens
They will make-do with what they have.
Exercising patience, they wait for something better
Committed to bringing order to a chaotic world.

If rest cannot be found for the best they give
Then rest they will not have, but it is for a reason
Their goal is to secure hope; there will be no rest for the weary.

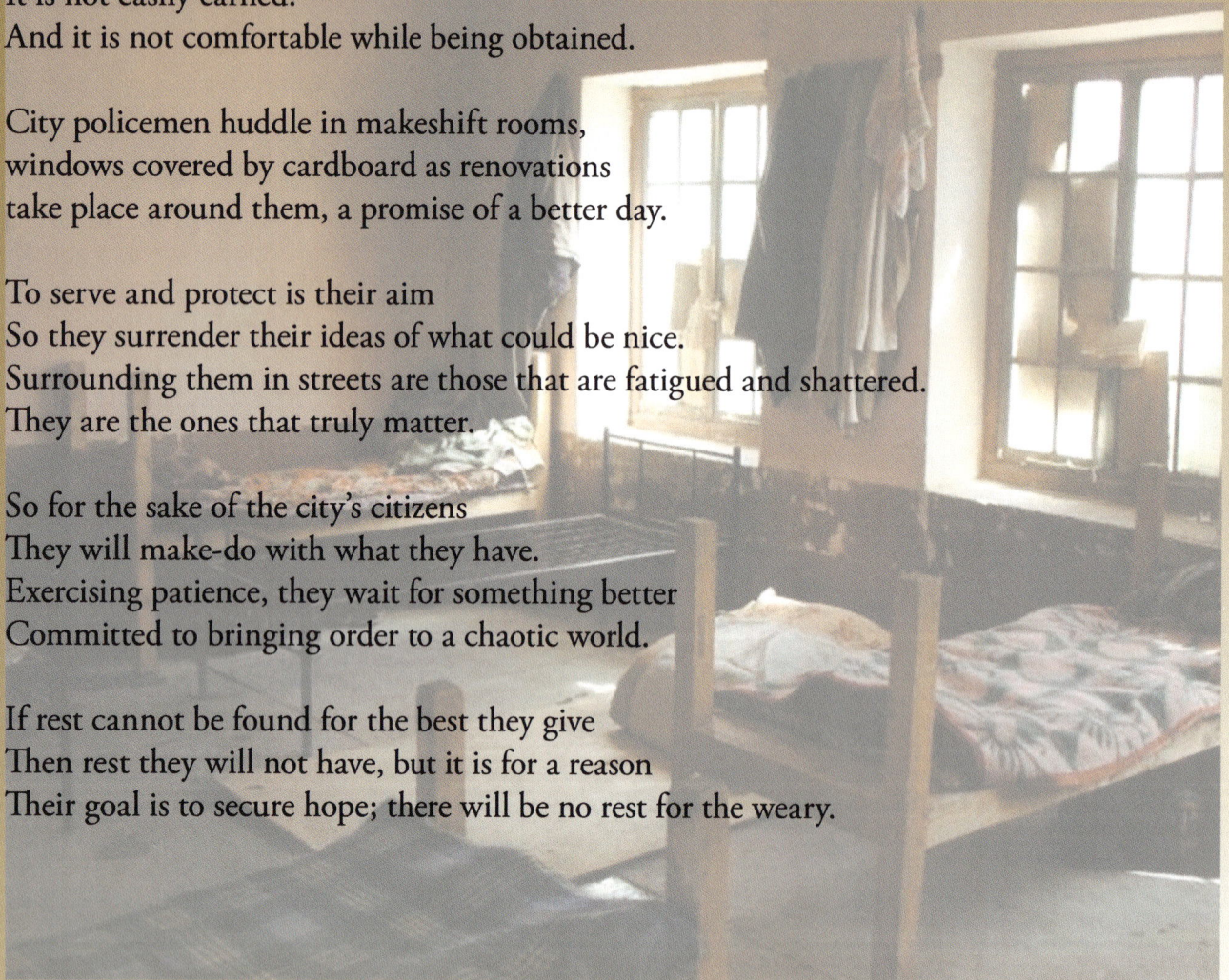

Not Today

This is one soldier that will not go down today.
While pain might rack the body
And somewhat maimed he may be; yet he will stand.

Wounded in various places, aided in his walk,
He will exit the scene. He will fight another day.
But not today, he will be out of commission.

Some call him gung ho, others call him motivated.
All he knows is that today, I will walk out of here.
I will see the sun set and hear another reveille.

Not today will they carry me feet first.
I will walk out of this situation even if I have to limp.
But I will be on my feet and not on my back.

And if someone has got to go and show their zeal
It will not be me, my commitment is to life.
And I will stay in the fight.

So if you think you are going to kick this anus,
Insurgents bring it on, come and get some,
But be prepared to pay the price, 'cause I won't.

So it won't be today that another KIA is added.
Not today that the body count will rise.
Today, this warrior will survive.

On Any Given Day

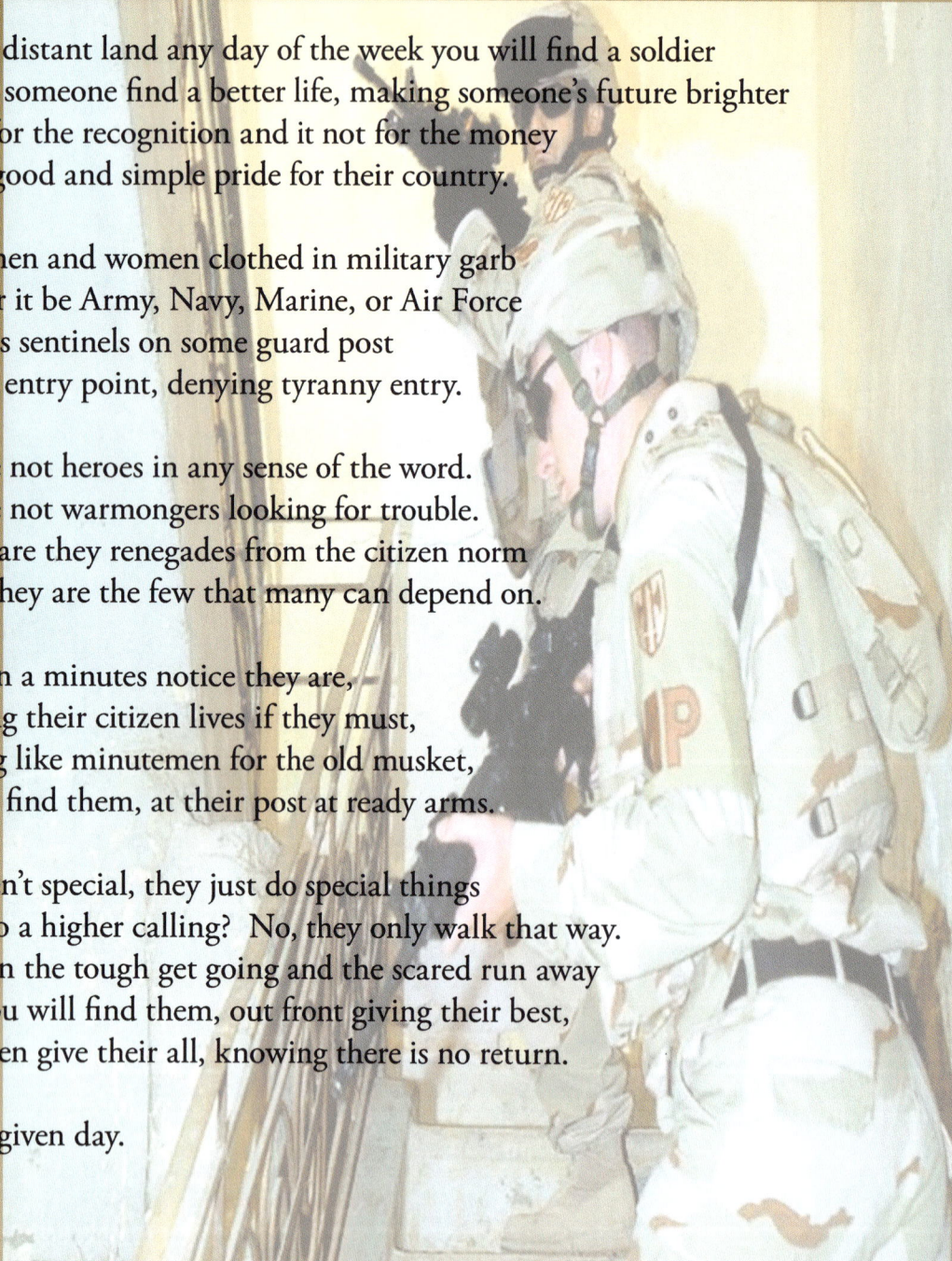

Somewhere a flag is flying, colors are proudly streaming.
Soldiers are courageously fighting for nothing else except
what they believe in.

In some distant land any day of the week you will find a soldier
Helping someone find a better life, making someone's future brighter
It's not for the recognition and it not for the money
It's just good and simple pride for their country.

Young men and women clothed in military garb
Whether it be Army, Navy, Marine, or Air Force
Stands as sentinels on some guard post
At some entry point, denying tyranny entry.

They are not heroes in any sense of the word.
They are not warmongers looking for trouble.
Neither are they renegades from the citizen norm
Rather they are the few that many can depend on.

Ready on a minutes notice they are,
Dropping their citizen lives if they must,
Running like minutemen for the old musket,
You will find them, at their post at ready arms.

They aren't special, they just do special things
Called to a higher calling? No, they only walk that way.
But when the tough get going and the scared run away
There you will find them, out front giving their best,
Some even give their all, knowing there is no return.

On any given day.

On the Wings of Angels

When mortar rounds starts coming in and
Everyone is taking cover
There is several wounded in action
That did not make it to a safe haven.

Worse still is when patrols are on the move, and a vehicle-improvised bomb explodes
Destroying the driver and wounding many soldiers.
It is then that help must be called to save their lives, suture their wounds and make them
whole again.

Dust off; dust off medivac at this grid.
We have wounded soldiers and the case is bad.
Can you get here quick and we mean fast.

A combat lifesaver is slinging IVs, tying tourniquets, and marking Ts on heads.
Our only hope is that the medivac comes quick so all our soldiers are not dead.

In the distance we hear it coming, and it's moving not so slow
It's the wings of angels, the medivac that is coming to get our heroes.

The wounds are bad, the medic is mad, he calls ahead for support.
On wings of angels they setup a rendezvous point
So the wounded can be taken to the CASH.

In the end, they saved our friends.
It was the actions that the medics took.
It was the wings of angels
That kept his name out of that wretched book.

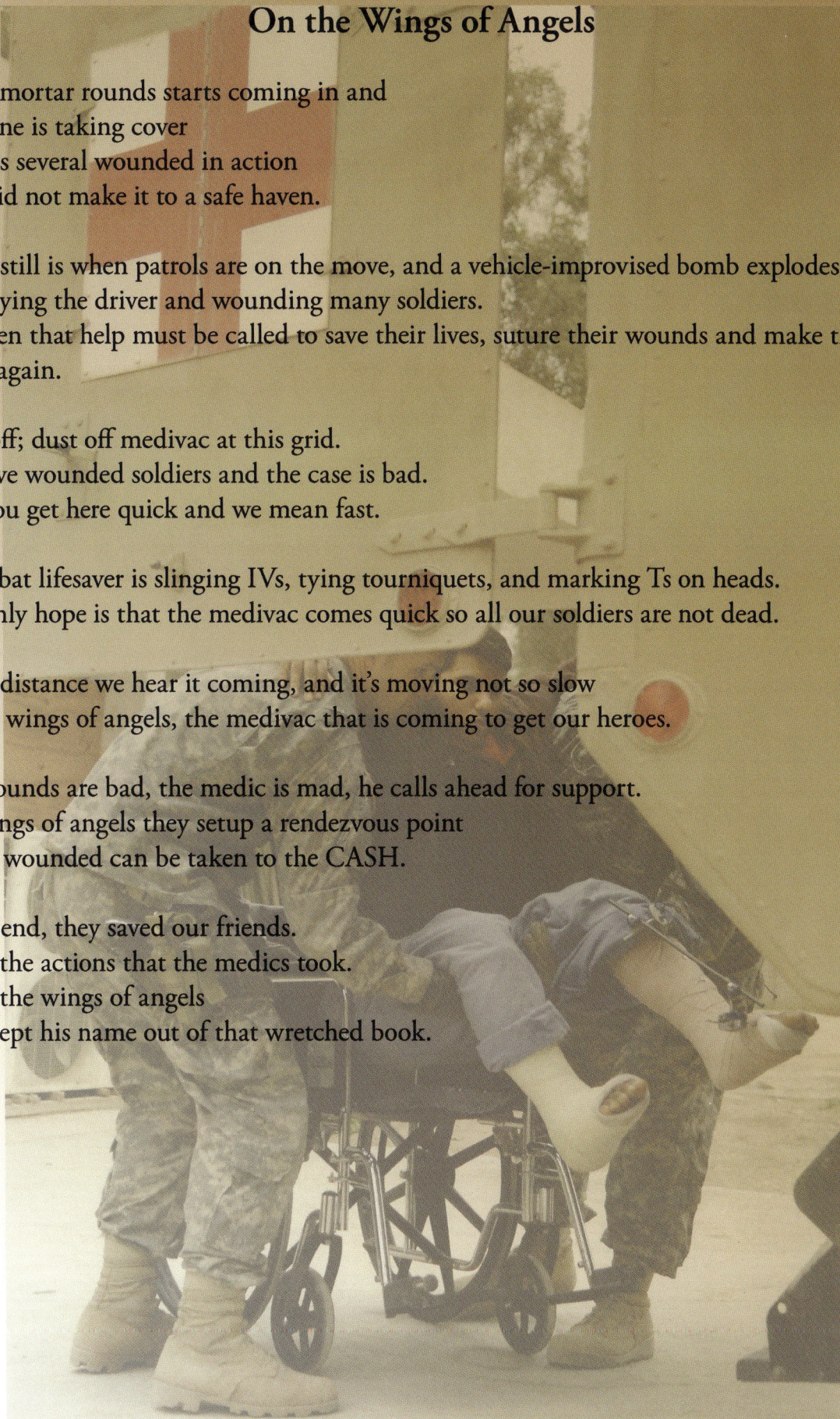

Only a Veil, Not a Shackle

What is given as her glory is hidden
Enclosed within a veil as if to hold down the glamour of the soul, forbidding it to smile,
keeping out the vibrant sunlight that would brighten the moment.

Why is the soul so suppressed?
Is that the way it was meant to be?
Are the features so homely that they must be hidden?
Or is the veil to mimic a shackle, not about the feet but the soul.

Through lifting of only a finger, speaking of only a word
A future is changed, a life is altered.
Hope is bestowed upon a new generation.
Above all, a smile is restored.

No longer is the veil a must, conforming to a statue.
It no longer has to hide the soul of the lady.
The spirit can now be free, letting the wind blow.
Freedom is more than a dream, it is now obtained.

So the veil is removed and the spirit runs free.
A frown is replaced and now a smile is displayed.
A heart is lifted and a tomorrow is made brighter.
It is no longer a shackle, only a veil.

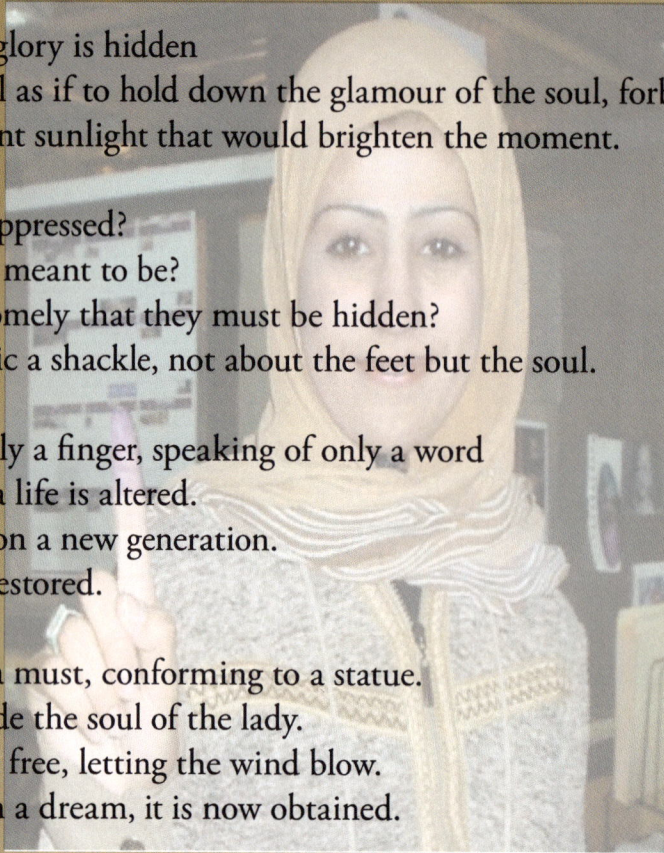

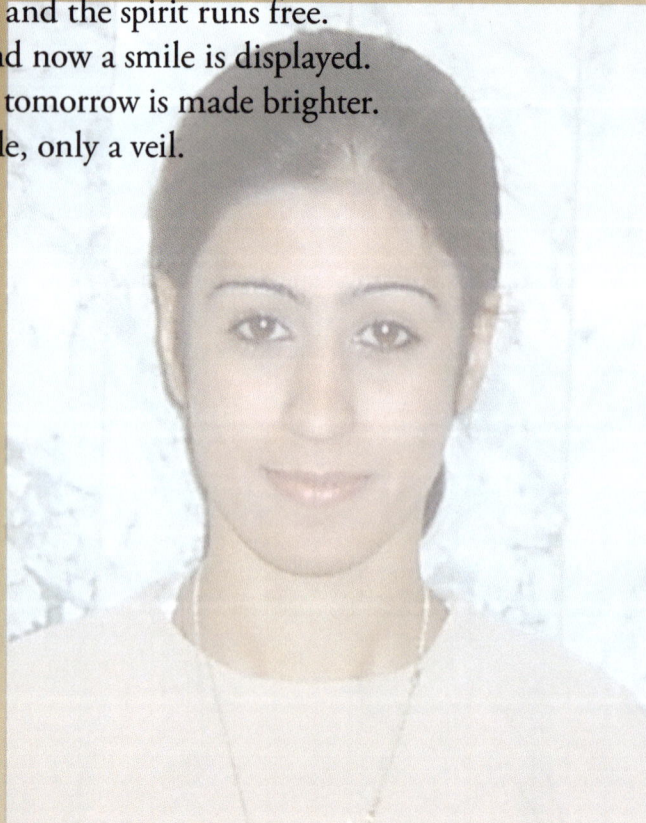

Perseverance for Sustenance

Determination is a matter of persistence
Going the distance, staying the course and keeping on track
To obtain the goal bargained for.

The haggling, the bartering to reach an agreement
This for that, more of that, give up a little.
Is it really worth all of that?

He has made his decision and he knows what he wants.
It is not a matter of giving in, only a means to an end.
No more dinars but just a few more leafy plants.
An agreement has to be reached or he will surely taunt.

With a few lower prices and more produce,
The jagged haggler has reached his price.
He has his goods. He is ready to go.
So down the street he strolls. Hands in pocket, he is satisfied.
He is headed back to his home.

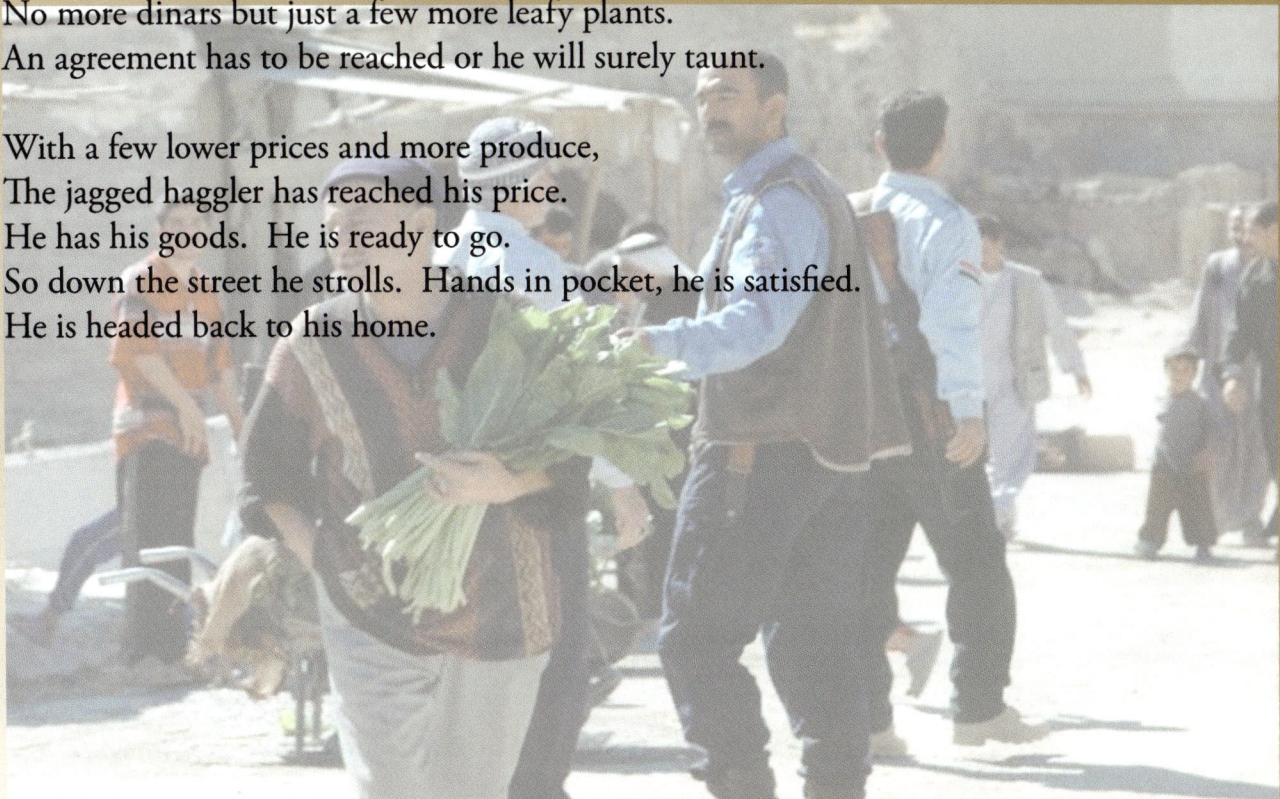

Please Bless The Child

With all the shooting and explosives going off
Everyone is running and trying to hide out.
Friends are covering friends, buddies covering buddies.
Everyone wants to see his or her friends make it home.

Weapons are loaded and everyone is ready to attack.
Platoons scout the parameters for sapper's traps.
No matter what the case of the situation may be,
One friend turns to another and asks, Cover me?

But in the middle of the search where a bomb exploded
A lonesome child is left all alone.
Parents are dead, few people are around, and all the medic can do is sit on the ground
holding the child in the safety of his arms, cuddling him close, keeping him from further
harm.

It's enough to treat a soldier who is only 18
But it is another to treat a child who hasn't seen a thing.
So what do you do? You just stop and say a prayer.

Please bless the child and not just the one I hold,
But please bless all the children, and let your blessings be bestowed.

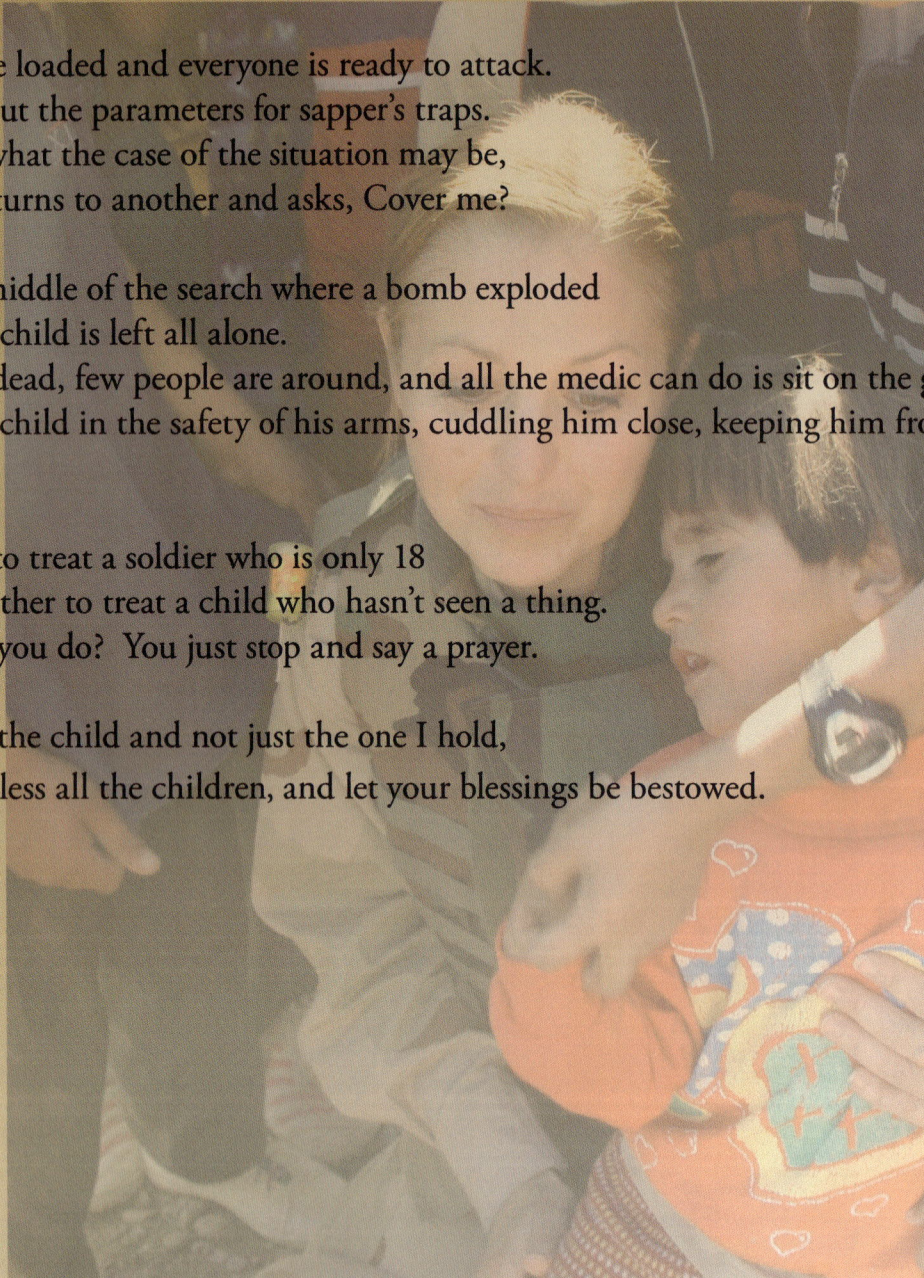

Purple Heart

Acts of bravery are very costly.
A squad pent down and one sole member draws the fight to himself to save his fellow
buddies.

Military Police in a convoy and the unit starts to receive fire
One NCO securing the move breaks off, puts chase to the ambushers, drawing fire from
the convoy and destroying the ambush party.

An Infantry soldier out on a patrol checking buildings for snipers.
Just as he kicks in the door, a burst of fire blows him out the doorframe.
Friends see the point man fall helplessly. Regrouping, they storm the room clearing it.

Sitting in a vehicle in a convoy moving down the supply route.
Weapons are ready, eyes fixed on the sides of roads looking for the unknown.
Out of nowhere an explosion goes off. It's dark. Slightly conscience, the passenger sees her
legs shredded.

These are the makings of acts of bravery.
Each price is paid in full.
Some are maiming, some are fatal, and some are just lasting scars.
But they all demand a purple heart, 'cause someone heart skipped a beat and bled.

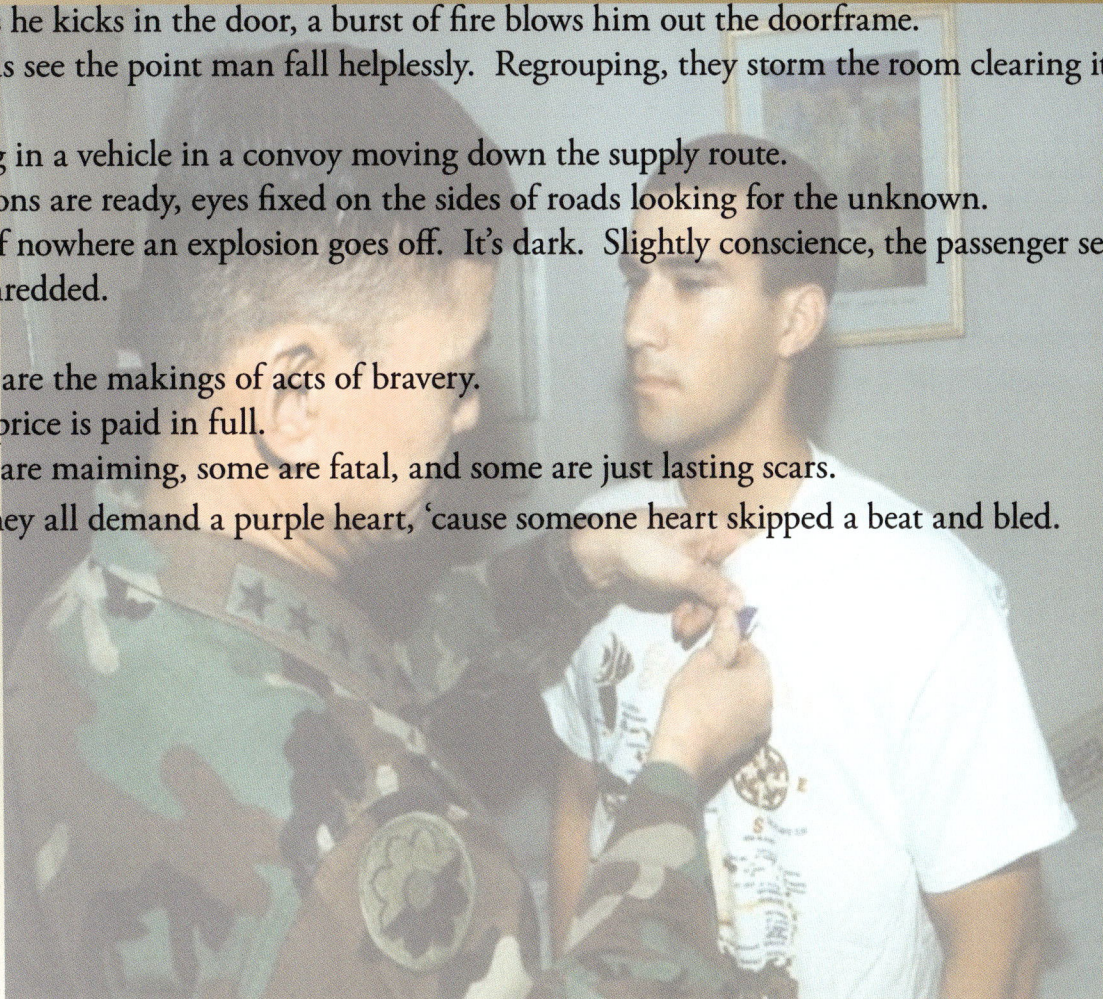

Saving Lives, Changing Hearts

It's not all about the trenches
With bullets flying overhead
It's more than winning conflicts and battles
The depth of commitment is seen in the success of locals.

There is a family that will sleep better without fear.
Another family will have meat with their meal just like those in a neighboring town.
Local citizens no longer have to be afraid of speaking out.

With the battle raging and death lurking around every corner
There must be something worth fighting for, some redeeming factor besides courage and
duty.
That factor is not based on any oath or promise.

In the eyes of the people on the streets
The local vendor peddling wares
Even the looks on the passers-by faces make statements
They are smiles, not looks of malice and deceit.

The lives saved are changing hearts
For every family that life has been improved, views have changed.

Soldiers fighting in Iraq are not just there to bring democracy,
They are there to make some family's life better.
And because their life is better, someone's heart is smiling…. not crying in the middle of
the night.

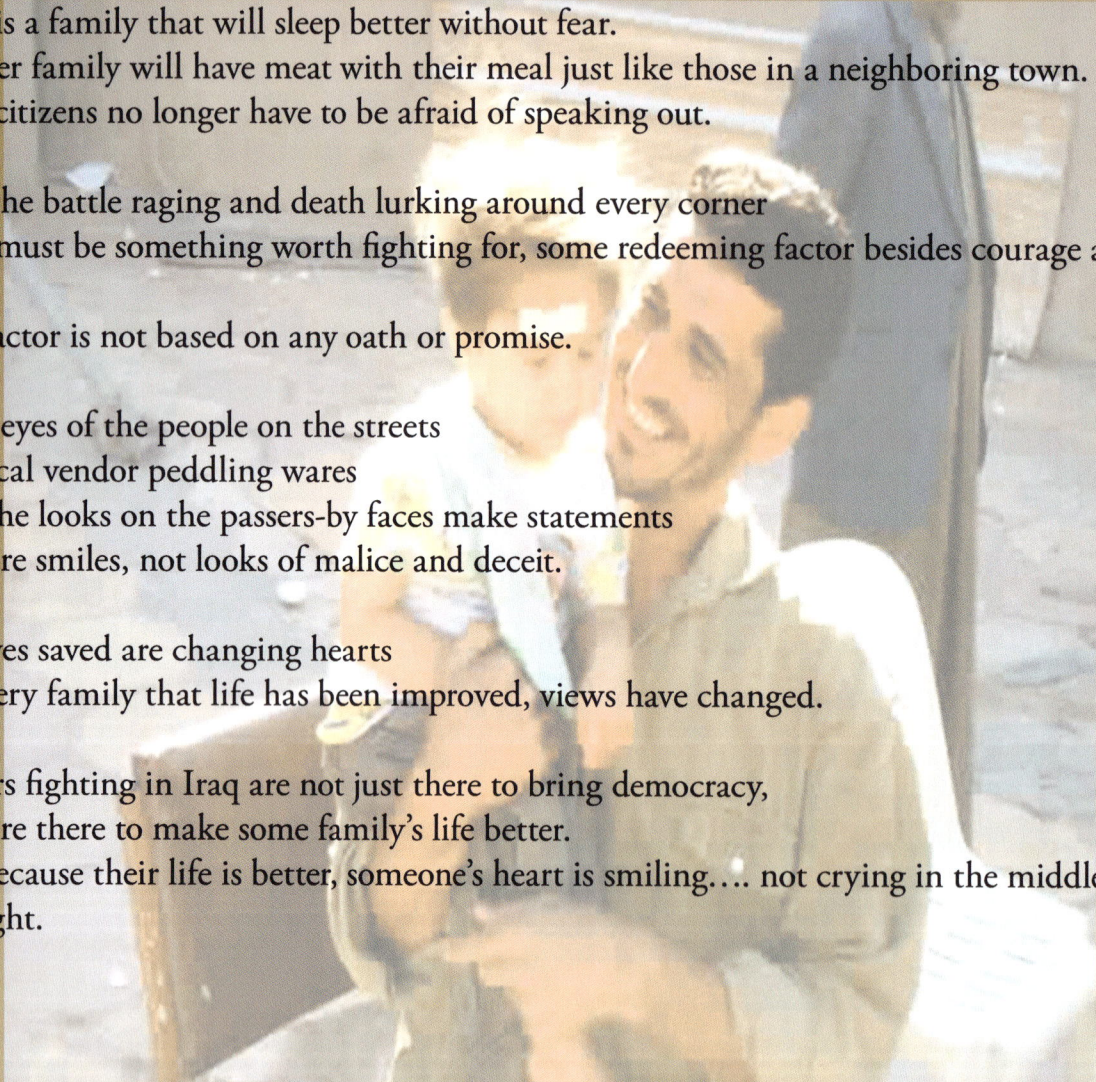

Sentinel On The Wall

On this watch she will not falter.
She will not sleep.
She will follow her first general order until she is relieved.

Her eyes are peeled for any movement outside the wire.
A twenty-round clip in the magazine well and
Another seven clips are ready to go.

Half-hour radio checks
"Hey base this is Papa four,
Its all clear in my sector papa papa four out"

But if there is a stray round that is shot off the flank,
shift from safe to semi and shoot in three round bursts,
put it to the enemy and make it hurt.

Not on this watch, not in this sector
There will be no breaches
There will be no false alarms.

There is a soldier on the wall,
a sentinel, and that soldier will not fall.
This is their mission and they are doing it day and night.
Their eyes are sharp and they are ready to fight.

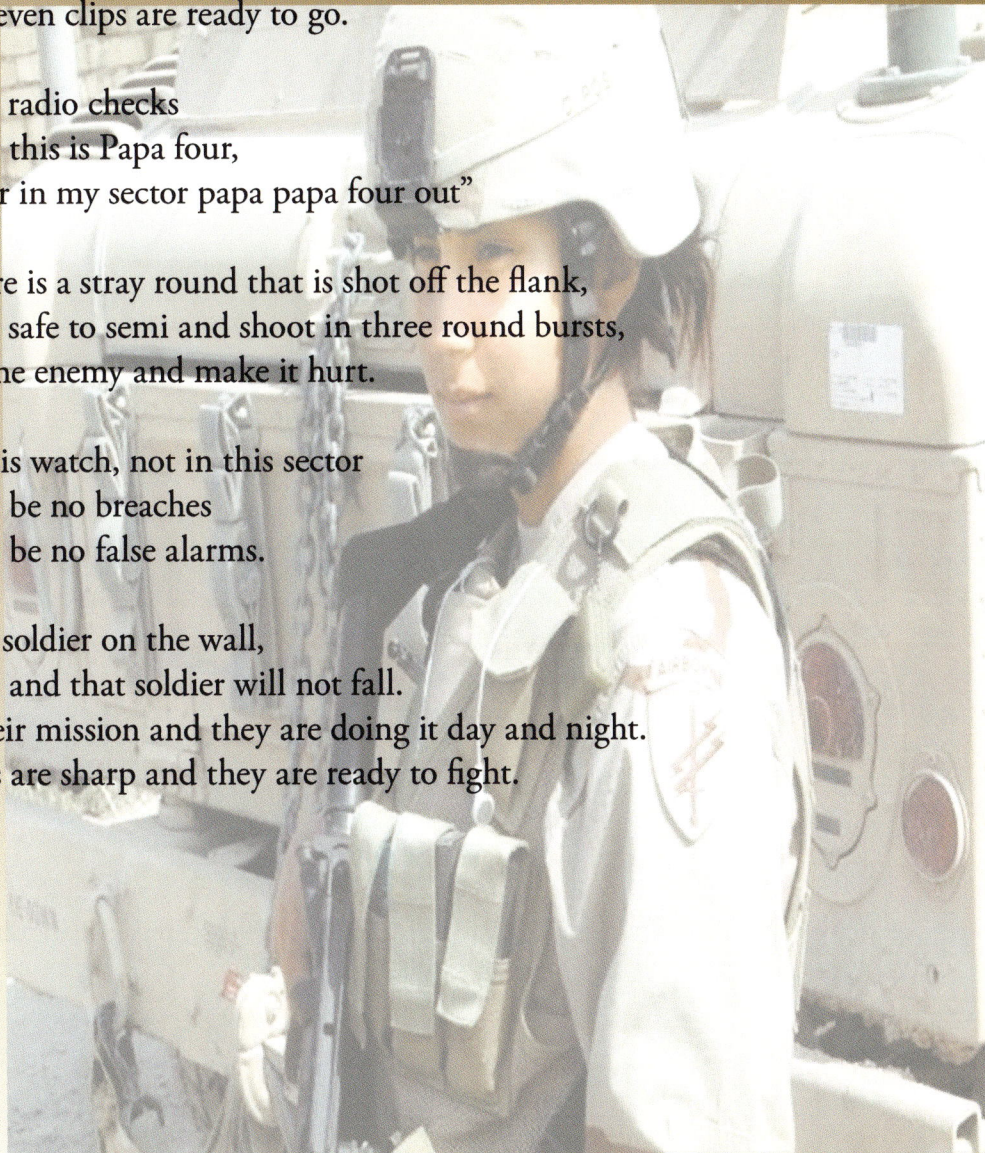

Serving With A Burden, Carrying A Smile

Everyone comes with their bags all packed
Carrying two and three suit cases
And other little knick-knacks.

Everyone wants to serve
to show how they support that soldier in the field,
Leaving love ones back at home
and problems that aren't sealed.

In the public's eye they laugh, so jovial they seem.
In the darkest night in the corner, they really want to scream.
The pain is far too great to bear
Not many know they even have a care.

Oh how well they wear that smile, so chipper they seem when they chat and joke, but deep
inside they want to choke.
In a foreign land they serve to support the red, white and blue
But in the back of their minds,
They are back at home fighting for the image of what was so true.

What seem like a long night with watery eyes
Is a moment past with a flood of tears.
Shake it off, shake it up and laugh it off like its fun
But there is more pressure building up than a bullet in a gun.

100% they are always willing to give,
helping others, lending hands.
Being a friend to someone else falling
Helping someone else to stand.

How do they do it, and never break a stride?
With a burden on their back, and a smile a mile wide.

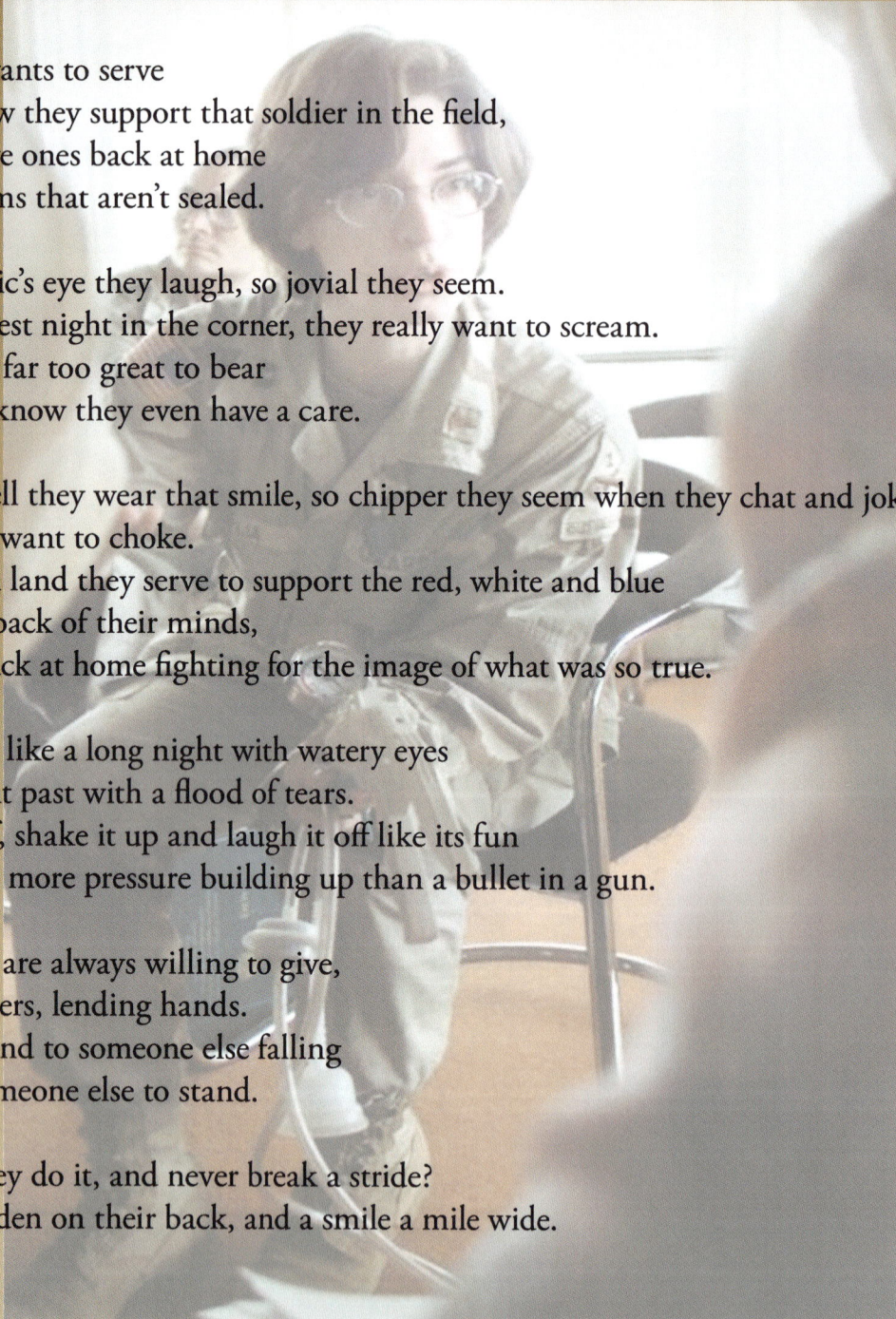

Silhouette of Hope

Everything is not always clear to the naked eye; rather it is only a shadow, barely discernible to true vision.

But for what is not distinctly clear, but just its outline, gives hope to those in despair. Along the distant horizon, images depict a backbone to a skeleton that stands strong.

When the battalion is on the offense and an ambush is hot and heavy, there is nothing better than to hear those rounds of hope land so strategically to force the enemy's hand.

Better yet is when follow-on units are receiving fire and it
seems that all hope is lost, but even though it is out of sight, its effect can be seen as it level assaulting fire teams and take out sniper positions that no longer clandestinely take out positions.

But as they roll back to their command posts
Setting up a small parameter for the night
Their tubs are aimed in the right direction
just in case they have to fight.

So as we see these shadows on the horizon
We know they have our back
They are our hope in tight situations
And our backup in a squirrelly fight.

Sister, Sister

Women do more than keep kids and cook meals
They are mechanics, crew chiefs, commanders and convoy leaders; more than sisters and
mothers.

While she may look good in them jeans, she is a killer in them DCUs. She is dangerous
with a machine gun in her hand and worse if you are on the other end.

She can run a two-mile in 12 minutes and knock out 85 push-ups in less than two minutes.
So be careful if you think she is only a pushover or it might be you she pushes over.

So after a long hard day of convoys, fighting bad guys, fighting
back ambushes and saving a couple of lives, Its just time for a lady to be a lady.

So sister to sister, one lady to another
each one knows what the other has gone through
So if just for a second, let me take a power nap. ...sister sister.

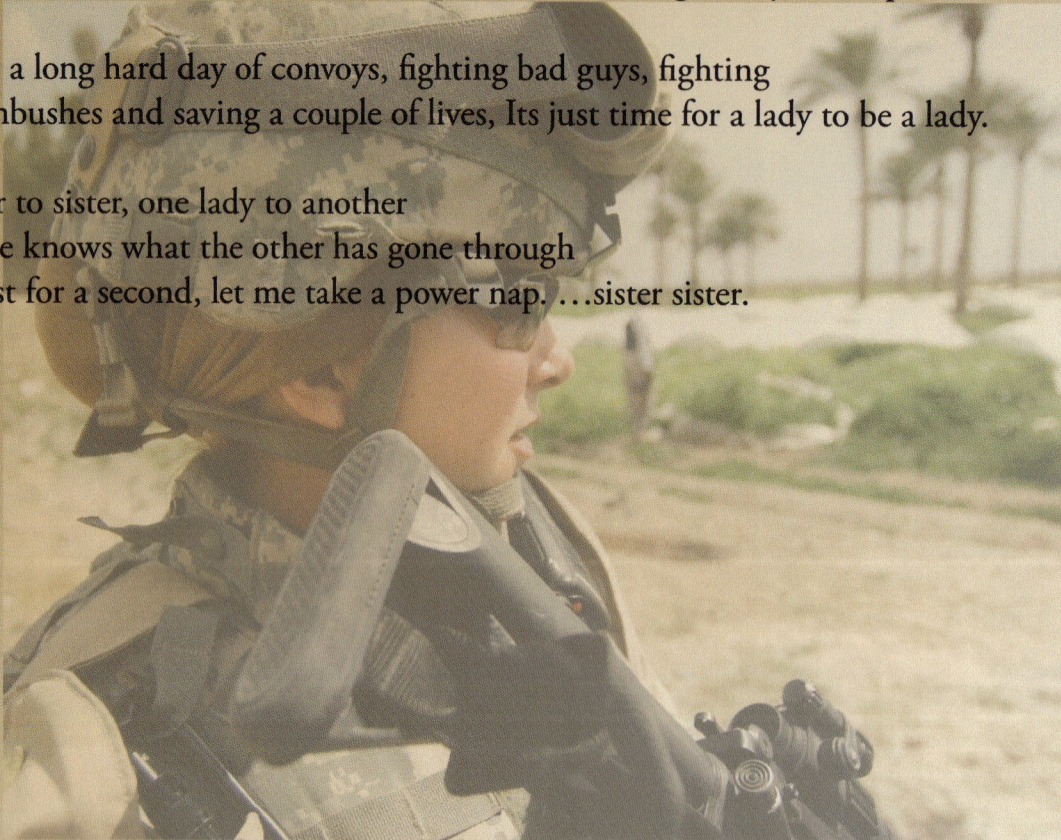

Smelling Home

Let me see, do I remember what that scent is?
Is that Diamonds, Red, or is it Opium?
Ahhh, that is the scent of home, of a sweet smelling lady 5'1, so fine, sweet, just right and just for me.

Ummm, is that her sweat I smell? If it is, how I do miss it. Wish I were there to take her all in.

After months of smelling musty men and sweaty feet and funk, after a long and hard day it is good to get this letter and be reminded of home.

The memory of how soft a lady can be might elude my short-term memory, but my sense of smell still works well enough to know how fine a lady is at home.

Snooze When You Can

What is an eight-hour day in the middle of a war?
It's more like sixteen hours or twenty at best.
So you sleep when you can in your helmet, boots and vest.

In the heat of a battle when rounds are coming in
You are too busy looking for cover,
Trying to aim your weapon and shoot to even think of rest.

So you clean your weapon when the firefight finally ends
Re-load your magazines, count all the rounds and check your gear
Doing a once over self-check from foot to ear.

Check the battle rhythm what must be done today
What is due out; what is due in
And what must be on its way.

By the time it is all done, 36 hours seem to be gone.
A hole in the sand is as good a bed as any, even if it's wet.
If you can only get a nap for an hour or maybe just two.
It will all be fine and you'll do it again when the first unit makes contact.

You can only run on fumes for so long before your tank runs dry.
So grab a mask or an old flat tire that you throw a poncho liner over for cushion.
Just a nap, that's all, til the next mission and we are called.

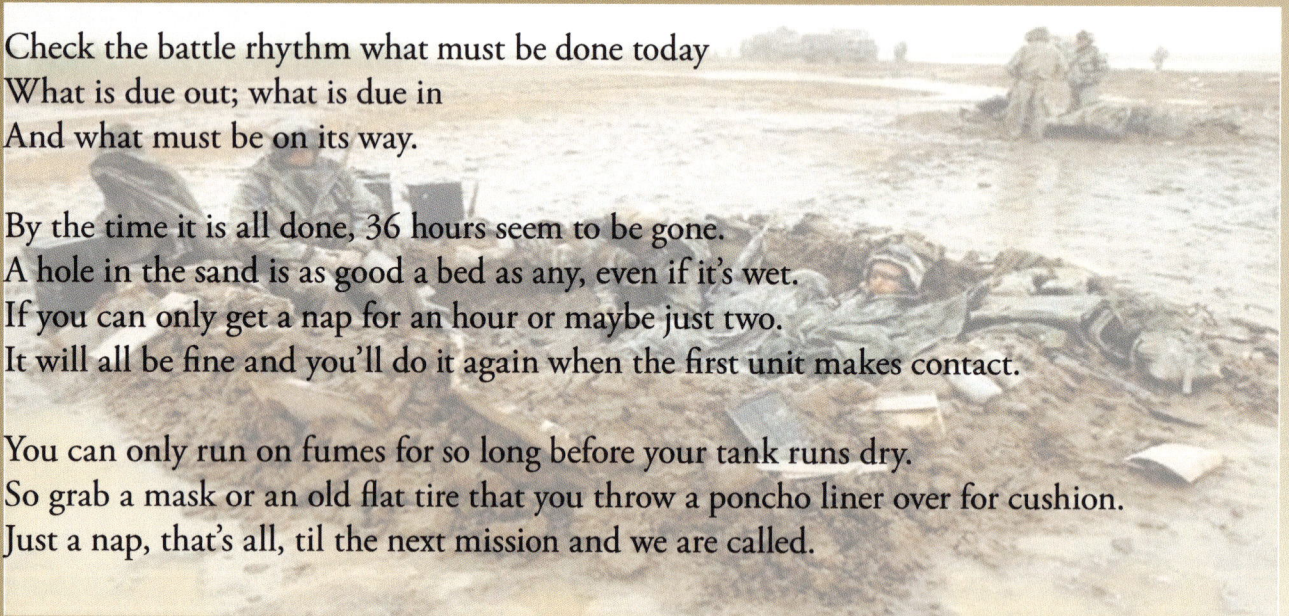

A Soldier's Sacrifice on the Table

What greater sacrifice could he have given than what he gave?
He made the promise, took the oath, stood to post, and
When the moment came, like a soldier he answered.

He gave his best to his family, whom he loved more than life itself,
A sweetheart that knew what love was and could not contain it.
They shared a romance that was sincerely fiery, and she will carry the memory forever.

His unit knew his dedication by the commitment that he gave
Always out front, ready to lead and an example to follow
Never a slacker, always a leader.

His comrades knew him as a soldier, one of a rare breed
Always willing to give of himself, the leader of the pack
He was a big dog; he didn't sit on the porch
He ran in the IED infested streets; convoying.

What was his purpose? To serve?
The willing committed to the unknown
In the midst of the uncertain.

His boots symbolize the stand he took.
His weapon symbolizes the courage he had.
His helmet is a reminder of his commitment.
And the flag is why he made the sacrifice.

His sacrifice is upon the table.

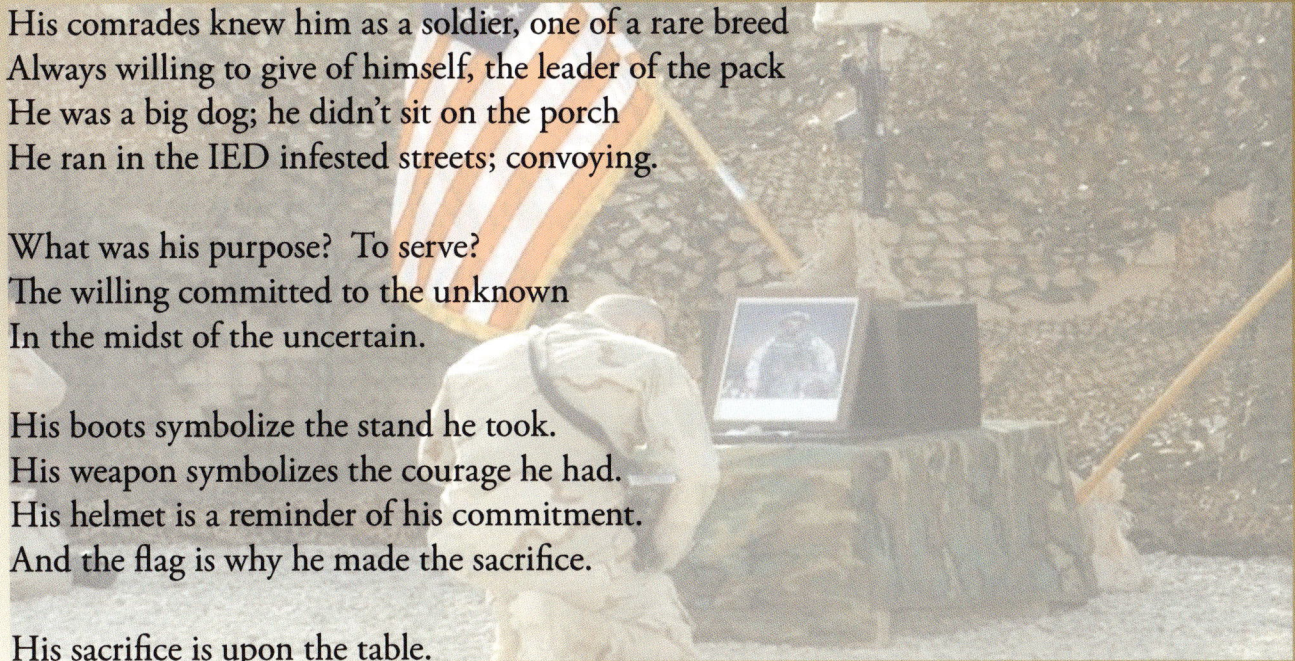

Soldiers out Front, But back at Home

Some talk about love of country,
The best words that are never spoken are actions.
Soldiers show their devotion to country by doing their duty with honor.

Many speak of loyalty,
But what is loyalty without dedication?
Out front, soldiers' lay their best on the streets.

Back at home they say they support our troops, but
It's more than signs and stickers on cars.
There is a soldier enduring sand fleas, camel spiders and leading our troops.

Some say they exercise their right to assemble by protesting
Out front, soldiers in the field exercise that right, standing in
the companies of fellow warriors in arms, fighting to get the mission done hoping to bring
everyone back home.

Back at home protesters "Asking for peace"
Stand to post, ruckup, ready arms and follow me.

Out front everyday, a soldier lays his offering at the base of the flag. What does he ask for?
Nothing. Just a country that backs him, politicians who support him, and fellow soldiers
by his side.

Out front is so different from being back at home.
Back at home, they can raise the banner, but out front they raise the flag.
Back at home they look forward to tomorrow; out front we are just glad to see it.

Solidarity

Extended hands from smiling faces eager just to touch
Rushing before a stranger that they have never seen.
Their fulfillment is just to feel and know this moment is real.

Oh, they have seen the soldiers patrol their streets
But those guys were serious and on the move
They were heading someplace and going there fast
With little time to stop and laugh.

But these folks, while dressed in the same thing that the soldiers wore, will talk with us and
shake our hands, and snap a few shots of us.
They seem so nice and ever so friendly, just maybe we can touch them.

So all in unity the hands converge
To reach a face that they have never seen
Their solidarity is to the moment and the kindness that the face brings.

Their urgent desire to converge on this visitor
One who they have never seen
Is a defining moment to their true identity
They like the changes that they see.

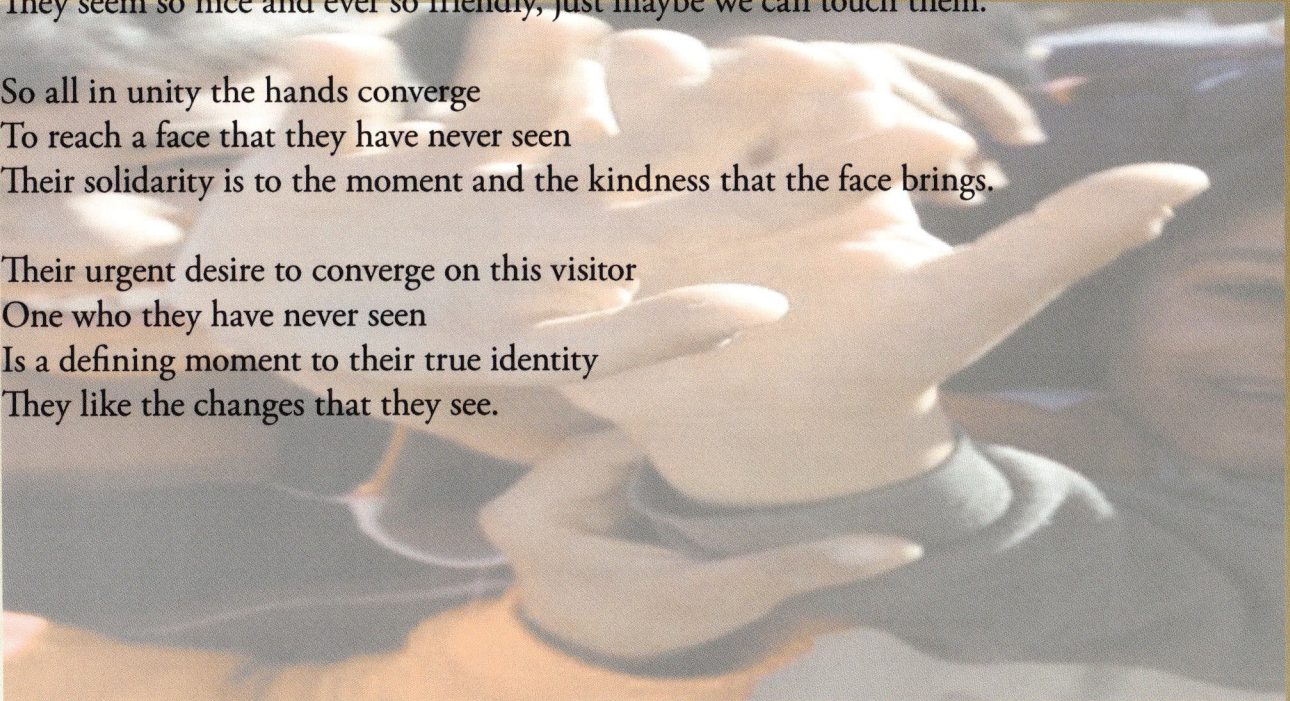

Somebody Cares

When the rush of the moment is gone and that time has past
Laying there replaying that moment over and over again
Visualizing the whole scenario repetitively 'cause it won't go away, like its on rewind.

With the doctors and nurses running around checking vitals
It seems like a whirlwind that will not stop.
Someone is coming in on a litter while someone else is going on another, and someone else is trying to calm another in the corner.

So when it all calms down and the litter urgents that are worst off are flown out for more critical help, and the place settles in a wild hum drum, it seem like nothing changes.

What is good to see is when someone from the unit, leadership, the division, or chain of command comes in to check up on you and see how you are doing, if nothing more than to say hello.

It's good to know that someone cares that another soldier is wounded, or that a troop from their command was injured and they stopped by to let them know that more than anything else, somebody cares.

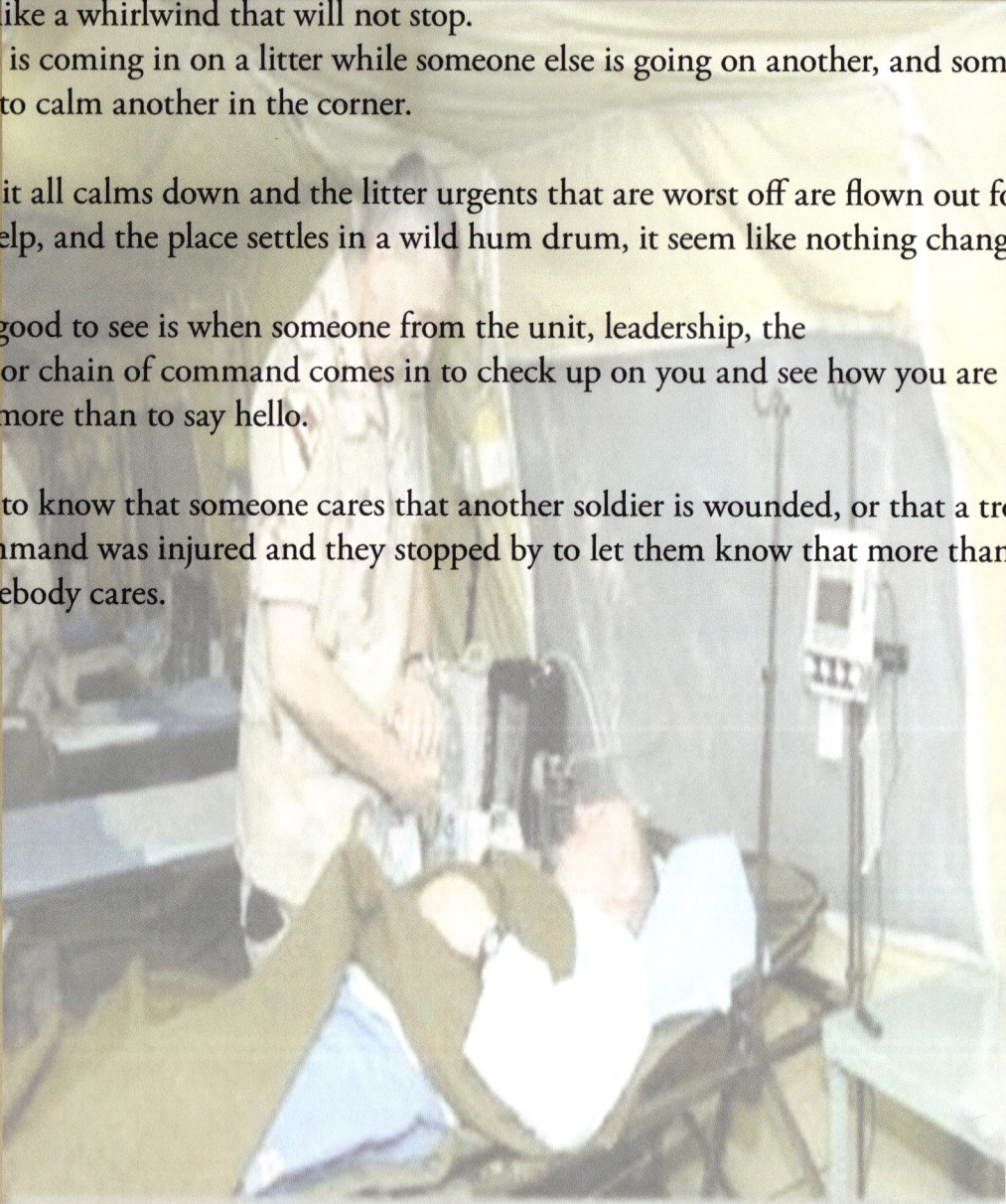

Standing for Freedom

Everyone has to stand for something.
What you stand for identifies what you believe in.
Called to arms, soldiers live and stand for freedom.

Eight weeks of basic training, learning there is no I in team.
Numerous weeks in advance individual training seals the initial philosophy.
When we reach our duty station, we are inducted into teams, sections, squads and platoons.

When called to arms to deploy and defend what every soldier
vows to do, there are no reconsiderations, no second thoughts.
If he believes in anything, then he must stand for it.

When asked would he stay for another tour,
Standing for what he believes in, he takes another tour.
Standing for the stars, the stripes and the colors.

The extended hand after a raised right hand is zeal of
my enthusiasm and my promise to serve and defend this nation
and all its interests.
It's my truest display of how I truly feel about freedom.

So what do I stand for; I stand for freedom!
More than words, these are my actions!!

Standing in the Gap for Hope

Who would dare stand for those under foot?
Who would give voice to those that are silent in their affliction?
Who would silence the tolling bells that bring sorrow to the listener?

The under trodden have seen what happened to the Kurds in '88
They had also seen the fate of those who dared speak out against injustice
Too often did they openly witness murder in the streets.

Those who bore witness were not only the middle age and aging
No, they were the young who had to live with those images for a lifetime.
They were the spirit of the young who would seek to find good soil and take root hoping for better days.

But as long as there was the icon of tyranny, all seemed hopeless.
Dreams were useless to have
Tomorrows were always the same
And the future was bleak at best.

With the roaring convoys rolling into town,
The soldiers building roads and schools, and giving away food,
Finally tomorrows are worth waking up for.
At last, the future has some hope.

The only reason things are better are because someone stepped in the gap between
hopelessness and hopefulness.
Where it was once dark, dreary, and trash infected
Now there is light, appealing and clean.

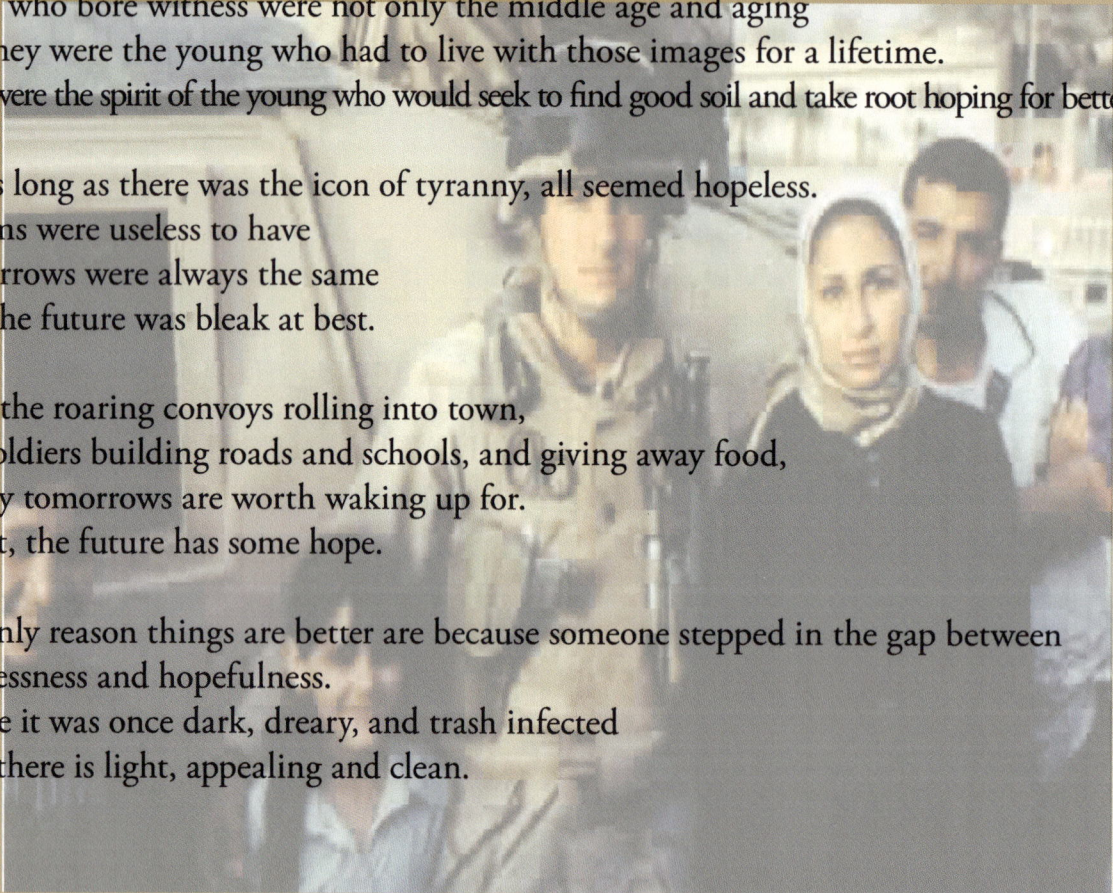

Strong Borders Make Safer Neighbors

How shall the children ever grow stronger
And never know the meaning of fear?
Not having to worry about insurgents that will kill the innocent by setting off bombs that leaves body parts seared.

All the neighboring countries deny what their people do
But with every roundup of new bad guys on the streets
Those stories just doesn't hold true.

Some slip across the Northern borders looking harmless as can be, but their intent is murderous, and their motives are not for the Iraqis good.

They just don't kill the men and women, but they kill the parents of kids that are young.
Look into a little girl's eyes and tell her it's not wrong.

Engineers combine their minds and focus all their might.
Building stronger border forts so they can thwart infiltrations and reducing the number that die in the fight.

Strong fences make good neighbors, but stronger borders make safer neighbors so families can live in peace.
So some little girl will have her dad when she is a lady, and a little boy can have his mom.

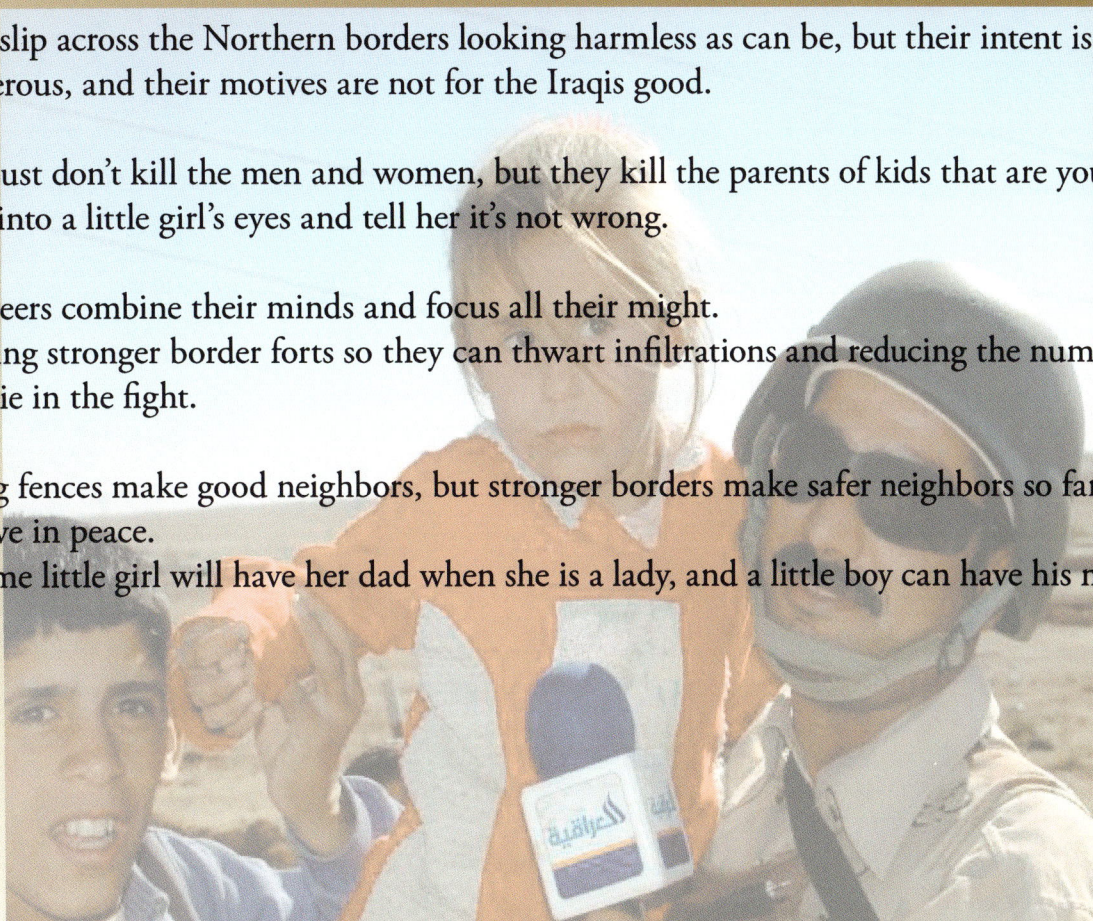

Sunset Over The Tigris

Another day the sun goes down and someone did not see it.
Looking across from the ancient river it really is difficult to embrace that this precious
moment is a repetitive motion in time and place.

How oft in time past have others stood on this spot
To look out across the Tigris to be taken by this image of old.
What were their thoughts, what were their hopes, were times just likes these?

The moment seem so tranquil,
Looking upon the setting sun.
Ancient Babylonians, Chaldeans and many more have viewed this sight before.
While new to some, it's as old as time itself.

The call to prayers swells across the evening air.
The sun, it slowly slips away
Calling the worshippers all to a moment of hallowed prayer
Before the close of the day.

And so this sight that was captured in time
Has been presented many times before
By a sovereign Creator longing for peace in this country of old.
This sight, in peace, shall be seen again.

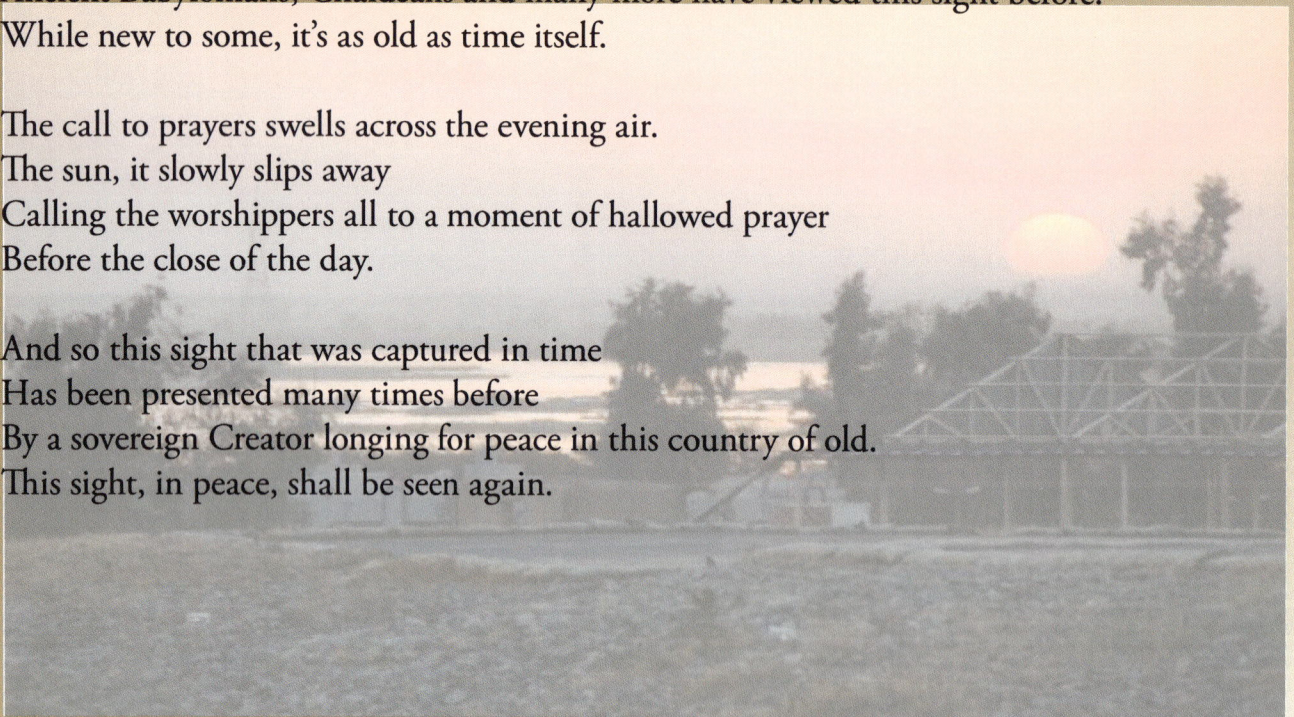

My Brother, My Sister, My Parent, My Friend

Soldiers stand ready to do what they are trained to do.
Defending their nation and doing what their President says do
Division commanders tell their brigades, brigades tell their battalions.
When it gets to the companies, NCOs push the schedule. Train soldier train.

Out to the fields they go and practice their craft.
Convoy ops, IED identification, force protection and ambush techniques. Everyone is
hoping that they are learning enough.
A lesson learned says that the insurgents are forever changing tactics.

All the soldiers are standing dress right dress
Filing from the left in a column left
Going through the lines processing to head into Iraq
Preparing for anything, some will not make it back.

Load all the equipment; after all hazardous cargo is marked.
All conexes are RF tagged and they are ready to go.
All flight plans are checked for the right number of PAX
Its pack it up, load it up, and put it on your back.

That soldier is somebody's brother, somebody's sister
Some child's parent and somebody's friend.
Everyone is hoping everyday that his or her loved ones will make it back home
Complete just as they left them.

Every face you see in some military uniform is someone
special in someone's eye.
Someone is praying that they don't get bad news such as a
special visit from the chaplain and you refuse to let them in.

They are not just soldiers, sailors, airmen and marines
But they are someone's family, someone's pal
They are someone special; they are servicing their nation behind the gun.

Tattered Doll

A dirty face adorn with a smile
A skinny figure is that of a child
In the ally she sits and stares
Watching the crowd pass, does anyone care?

Her eyes tell a story that is sad indeed,
In tattered clothing, no shoes and a wool cap upon her head,
This child search the faces of passers by
looking for hope to remove the dreadfulness.

A doll she is beneath the dirty smear
Gaze upon her and see her messy oily hair.

Whether it is hot or cold, it remains the same
Hopelessness drapes her shoulders and despair
 is about her mane.

With the rising sun she sits in the same place
Where she was before,
Lying in front of a storefront door.

In the blazing sun, in a box she hides.
This tattered doll with potential so great
No one will ever see what all she can be.

Day after day there is no change,
Year after year it is just like the year before,
the same.

For all that she could've been
And all that she could've seen will never be.
As a tattered doll before the eyes of the world
This little girl will always be.

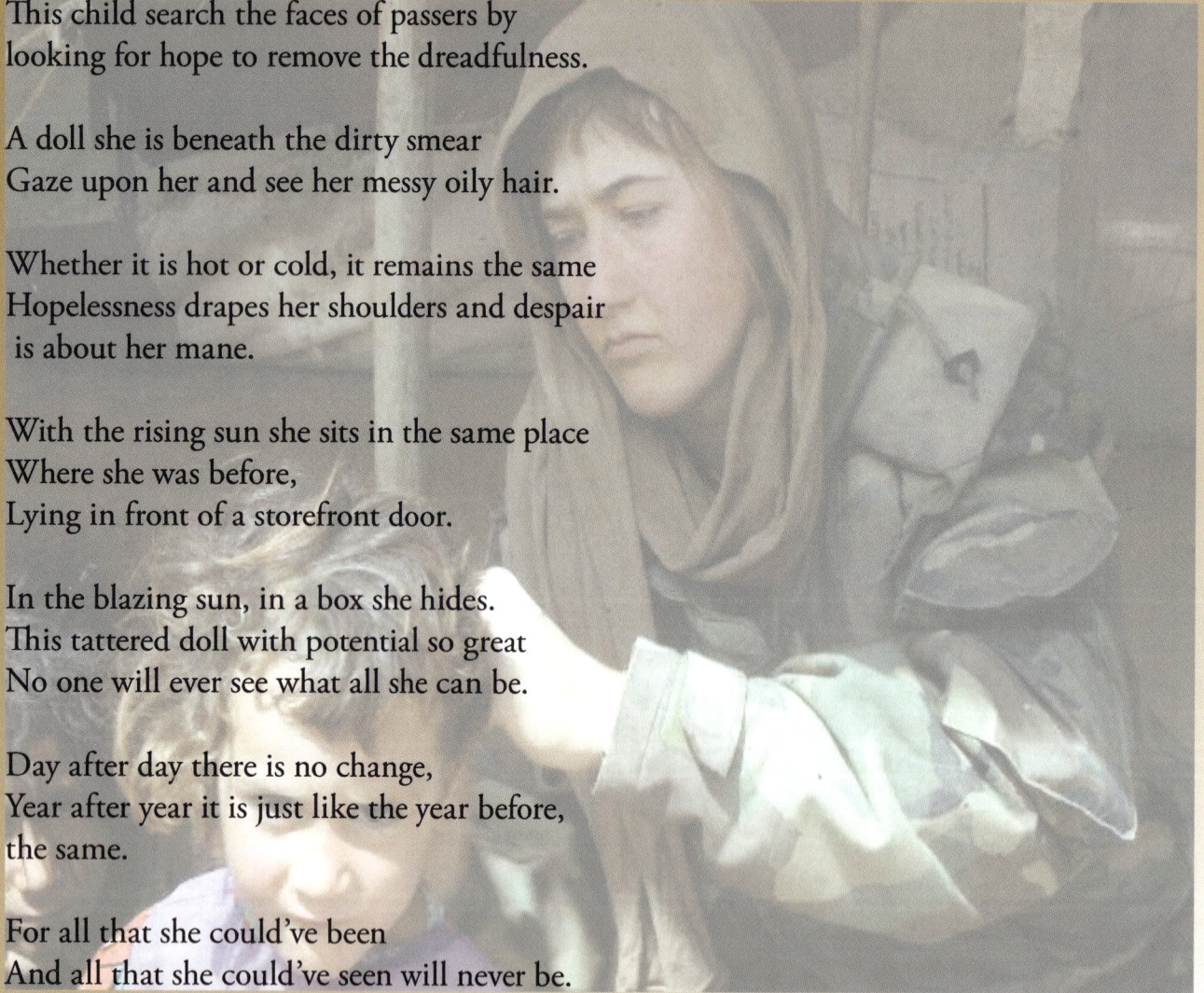

Tears of Remembrance

Before a helmet that will never be worn again,
That stands upon a weapon that will never be carried again
Between a pair of boots that can never be filled
One good man among many men shall be remembered.

Crowds of folks are assembled to recall the sacrifice
Men and women in uniform looking distinguished
wear a stern look upon their face and when they pass each other they echo "Semper Fi".

Looking upon this scene there is a matter of knowing
that each one went down fighting but standing up.
The pain will well up from the deep, knowing there is no return from this rest.

The pride in this moment comes from knowing that
this helmet did not belong to just anyone, but to someone special, someone dedicated to
more than just a family, but to his country, to the corps, and to his unit.

While he cannot be taken beyond this sacred ground,
These tears will mark this spot, this moment and this pain
His going was not in vain; it was for a noble cause.
These tears exemplify how he was more than a father,
To a son or a daughter he was a friend,
He was more than a husband or a son; though he was dependable and reliable.

He shall be remembered for his strength
He was a soldier, a marine, a true American.

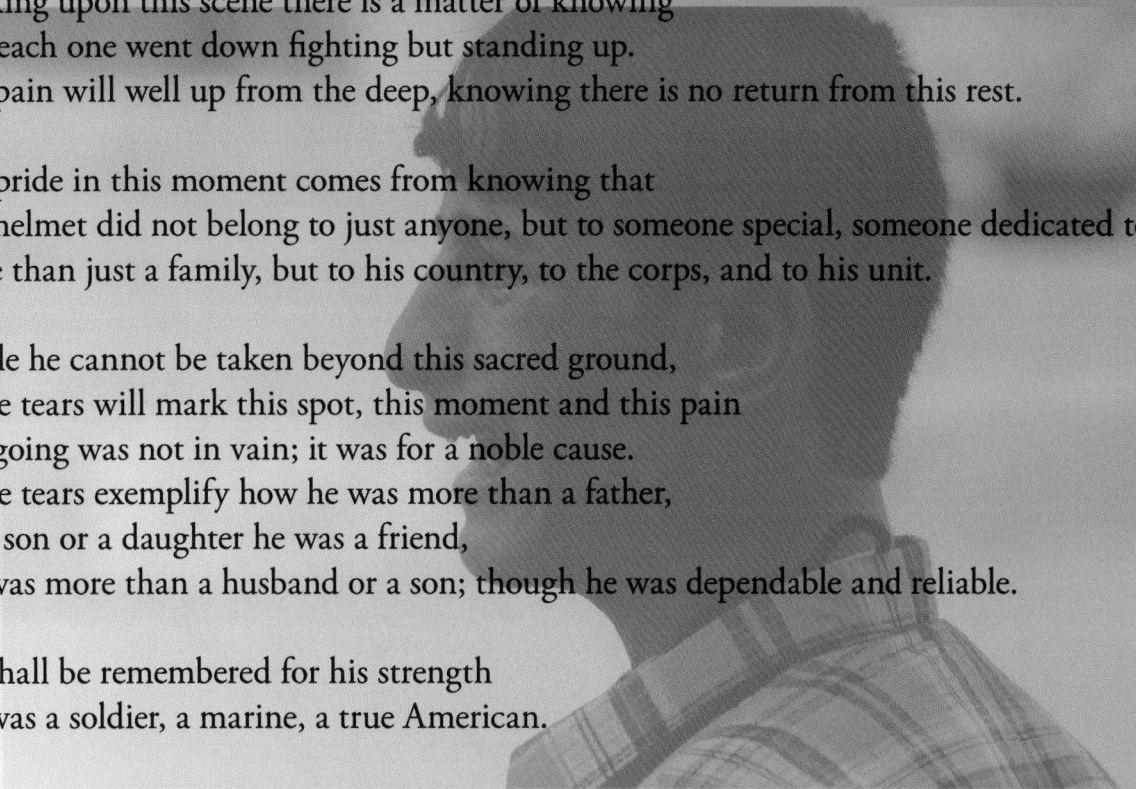

Technology on the Battle Field

It is not as simple as it use to be
When the idea was that the battlefield was linear
No longer linear, the battlefield is everywhere and
that idea can stir up a scare.

We no longer have PRC 77s radios
But we have the new RT 1593s
They are more than a radio
They can take you where you want to go.

We have GPS and UAVs
And other things that old soldiers have never seen.
From Stryker Vehicles to Foxes
But they are rolling and setting up roadblocks.

We have night vision goggles to see at night
And other devices that make night seem like daylight
That is just the tip of the iceberg.

We can track our forces
We can track our guys
We can even see what our guys see
Now that technology is what we call neat.

The battlefield that we are on today
Is not the one of old, no way.
It is newly fangled, signal triangled
This battlefield is all wired.

Because this battlefield is all about technology
And tech doesn't' get any better than this.

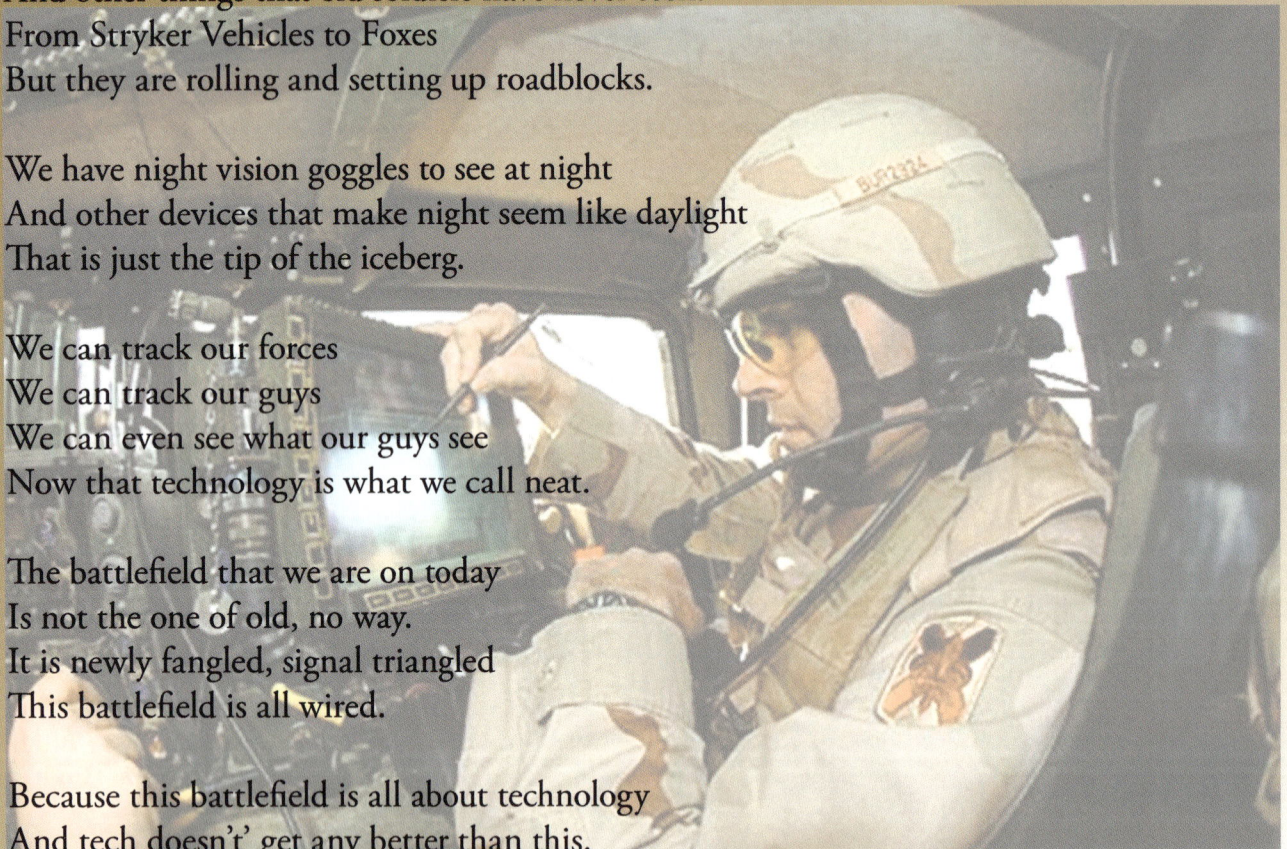

Thankful For The Sacrifice

For as many that have come from such great distances
Their goals are the same
Restore the peace, give hope to the despair
Above all, build up the torn down.

The willing choose to give
Not by demand, but because of dedication.
Dedication to duty that exceed our local philosophy.
Dedication to honor that is doing what soldiers have always done.
Dedication to country that exceed our boundaries.

It is more than what our country is to us.
It is what others countries are to them.
To the orphans we want to be protective parents
To the destitute we bring solvency.

It is our pleasure to serve
Through our sacrifices, perhaps we lessen future sacrifices.
Your children will know peace, not tyranny.
Women will know hope where it was once unforeseeable.

So when you see that flag wave
Just remember this is what we live for
So that you have something to live for.

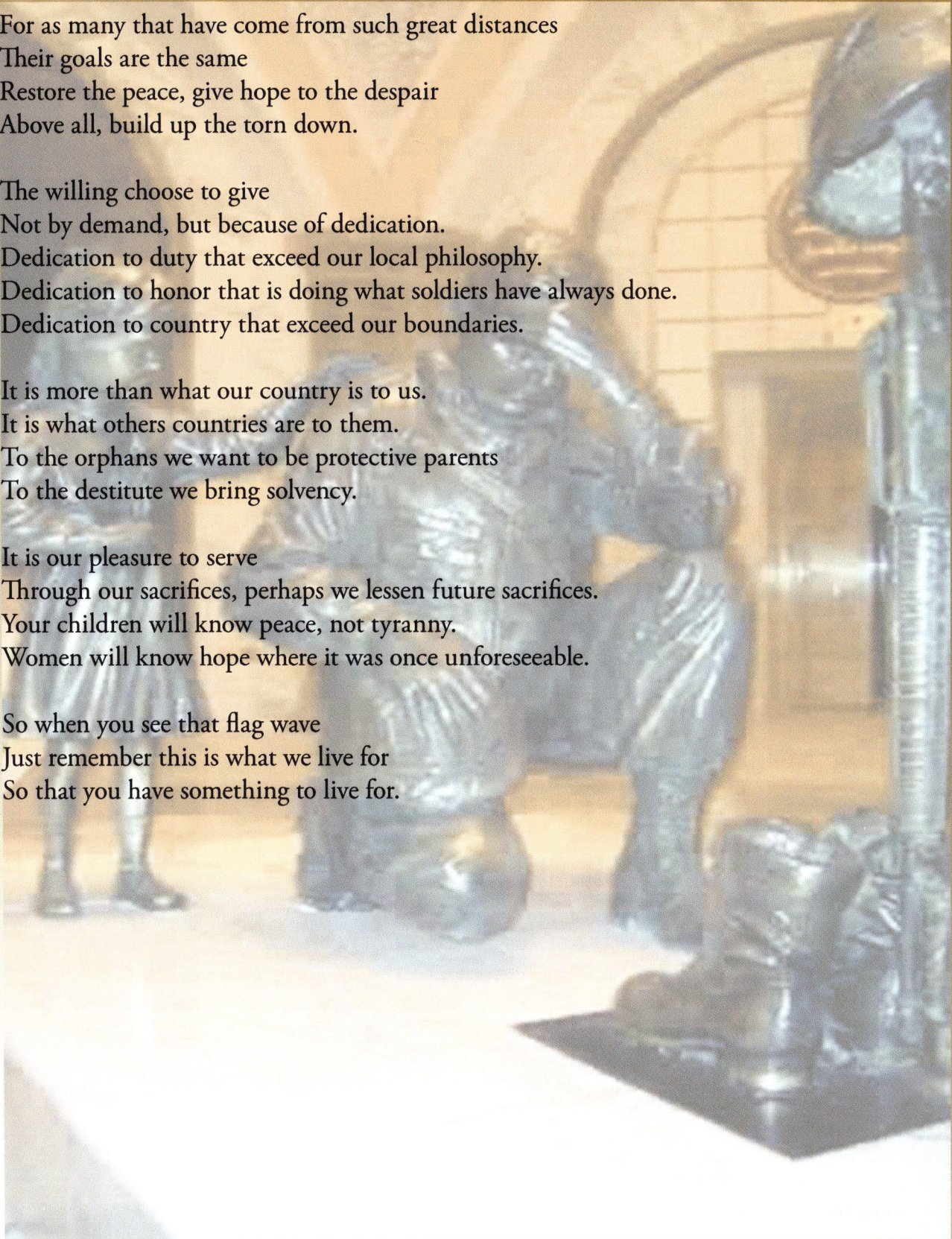

The Freedom Lamp Is Lit

Freedom never came without a price
Someone has always had to paid the toll
So other could enjoy it.

The battle in Falluja where Marines fought tooth and nail
One street after another, IEDs all over the place.
But they stood there; a few good Marines secured the place.

In the ancient city of Baghdad where insurgents rocked the streets, the
1st Cavalry Division held their ground and took the city corner by corner,
and road by road. They had their share that paid the ultimate price but the Cav rode on.

When the insurgents were running rampant in the city of Mosul, the 1/25th Stryker Brigade
rode like a "ghost rider" through the streets where they ran to and fro, and many offered
their oil, but they never stopped rolling and they forever stayed in stride.

So they said that the lamp of freedom must often be refilled with oil from those willing to
make the ultimate sacrifice so that the light never goes out
The light in the lamp is burning rather bright these days.

Day after day, more oil is added to the freedom lamp as one of our Sentinels fall, offering
their oil to the lamp.

We shall guard the lamp with our lives; the freedom lamp will not go out.

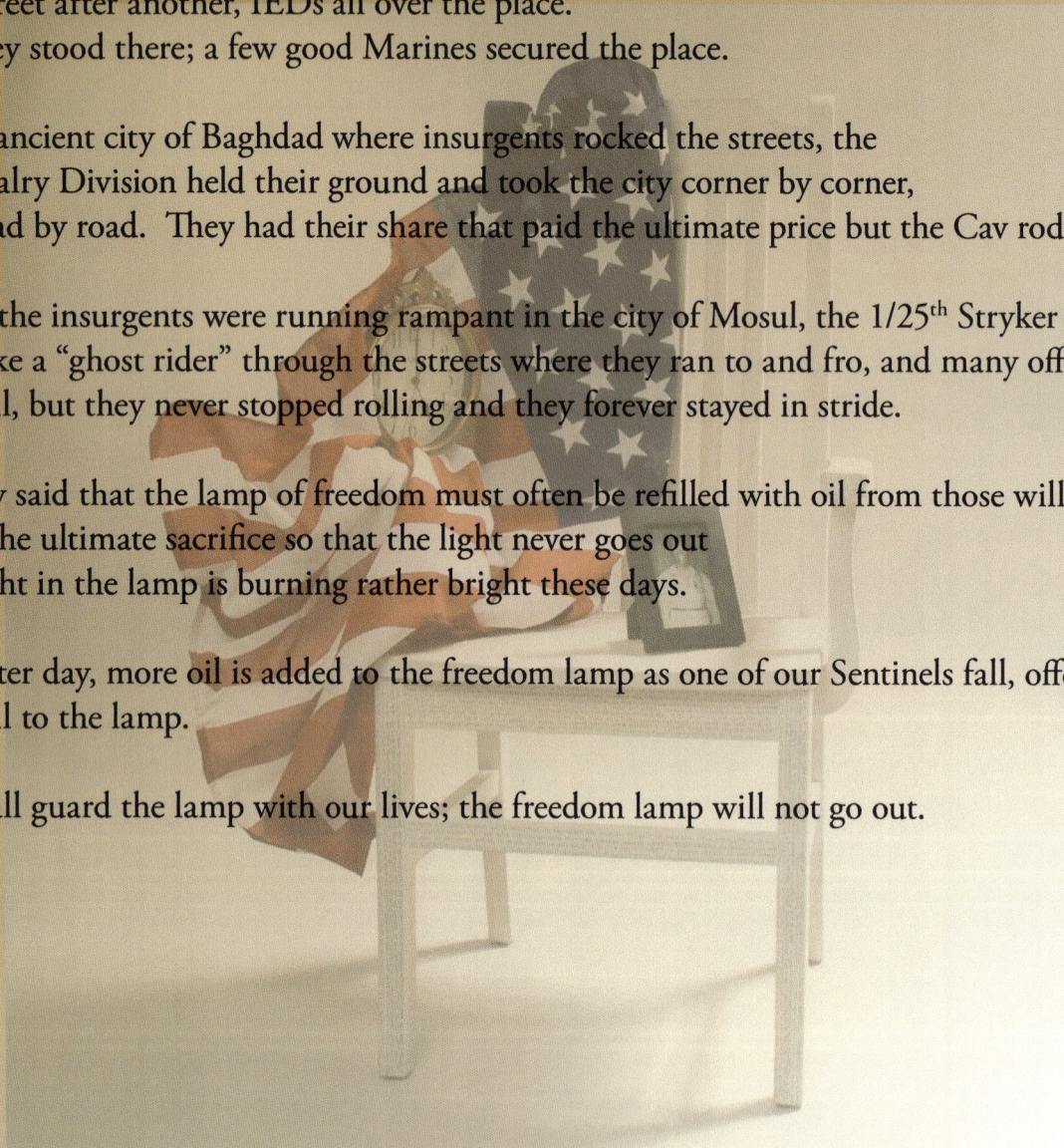

There Is Strength In Numbers

One is a lonely number when you are trying to fight for life.
Two means your back is covered, but it's up close and personal.
Three adds some dimension to the equation, now you have a spotter.

I never was strong enough to hold them off.
But we do a heck of a job kicking butt and taking names.
It's a numbers game. The more of us we have, the more of them we will stop.

It's really quite simple, because if one can defeat a thousand, then two
can put ten thousand to flight.
The greater the number, the greater the cumulative faith in one another.

If I am my brother's keeper, then my brothers are a full concert band;
each one with their own specialty, their own dedication, their own commitment.
It is no longer one by one, but together we stand or divided we fall; so we stand together.

The numbers are not separated by gender, race, religion or nationality.
We are united because we believe in the same thing and we believe in each other.
You trust me and I trust you, which makes two. Now multiply it a thousand times.

In numbers there are masses and great masses total large numbers.
So we are a mass covering each other's back, remember that
You got my back and I got yours.

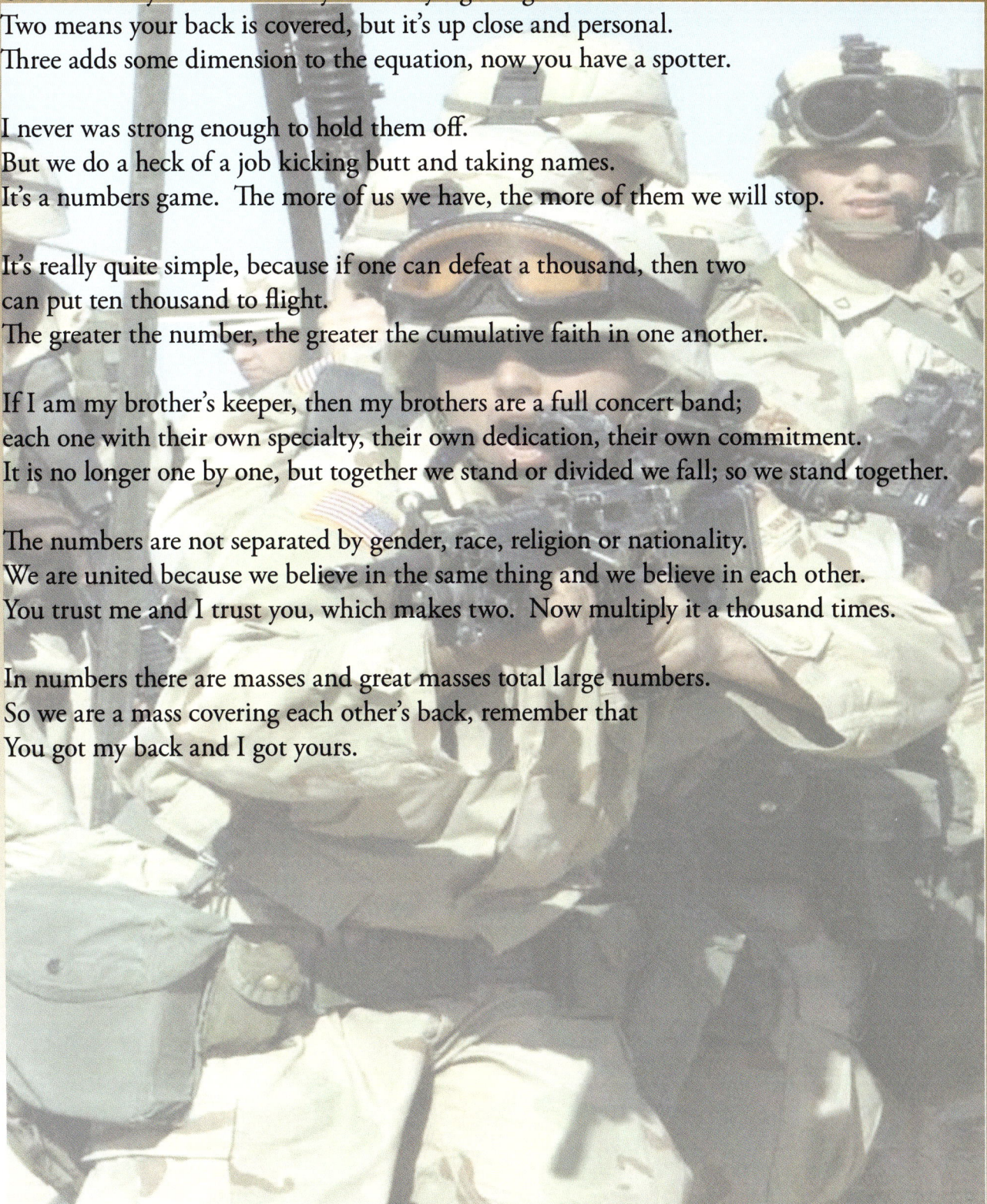

Too Often The Innocent Pay

What humble soul lie resting in open arms
Too innocent to know evil, too frail to defend.
A lifeless form, it would surely seem
Certainly a small body reeking with pain.

What is her crime? Why must this be her fate?
Is it merely a reflection of where she was born
that sealed this day?

Was she in the wrong place at the wrong time?
Too happy for the moment?
Or maybe she just didn't see it coming…
So the innocent must pay?

Who will shed a tear for this soul?
Who will count one less chair at the table?
Who will wonder why this card and not another were dealt?

On-lookers eyes will swell with tears.
Open arms will carry her to a place where hopefully she can be healed.
But just in case the tears soothe no pain.
Just in case there is no hope to be gained.

All who see her will surely know
That this battle we fight is not about her
But rather those extremists who take her from love ones will cease to be
She was taken for no other reason than her innocence.

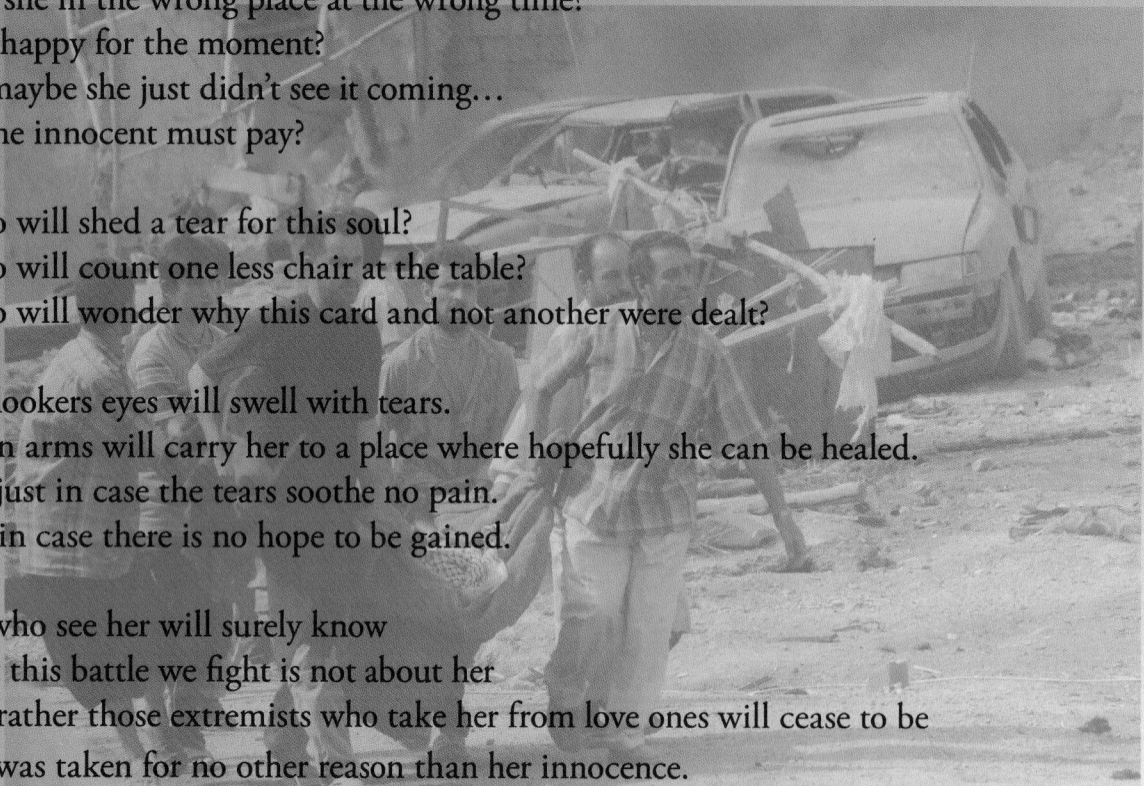

Today's Views, Tomorrows Hopes

Whoever said that you couldn't see the future?
Never looked in the eyes of a child who only
knew pain, and suddenly saw hope in the face of despair.
Where once a grim face, now they awaken each morning with a smile.

No one has to tell them to smile for the camera.
It is not a cameo moment but a moment of truth.
They do not live in fear when they awake.
They do not dread the night when they go to sleep.

For today they see freedom in the streets.
Tyranny is not in rule anymore.
Death does not trample the streets with fear at its side.
Not anymore,

Market centers are being rebuilt
Schools are restoring self-recognition.
Democracy has been chosen.
Tomorrow is truly hopeful.

A child can look forward to being an adult.

They can dream that impossible dream.
When they look up and see planes flying,
they actually can dream of flying them one day.

Yesterday is no longer an image of tomorrow.
But the view they have today is the hope they have for tomorrow.

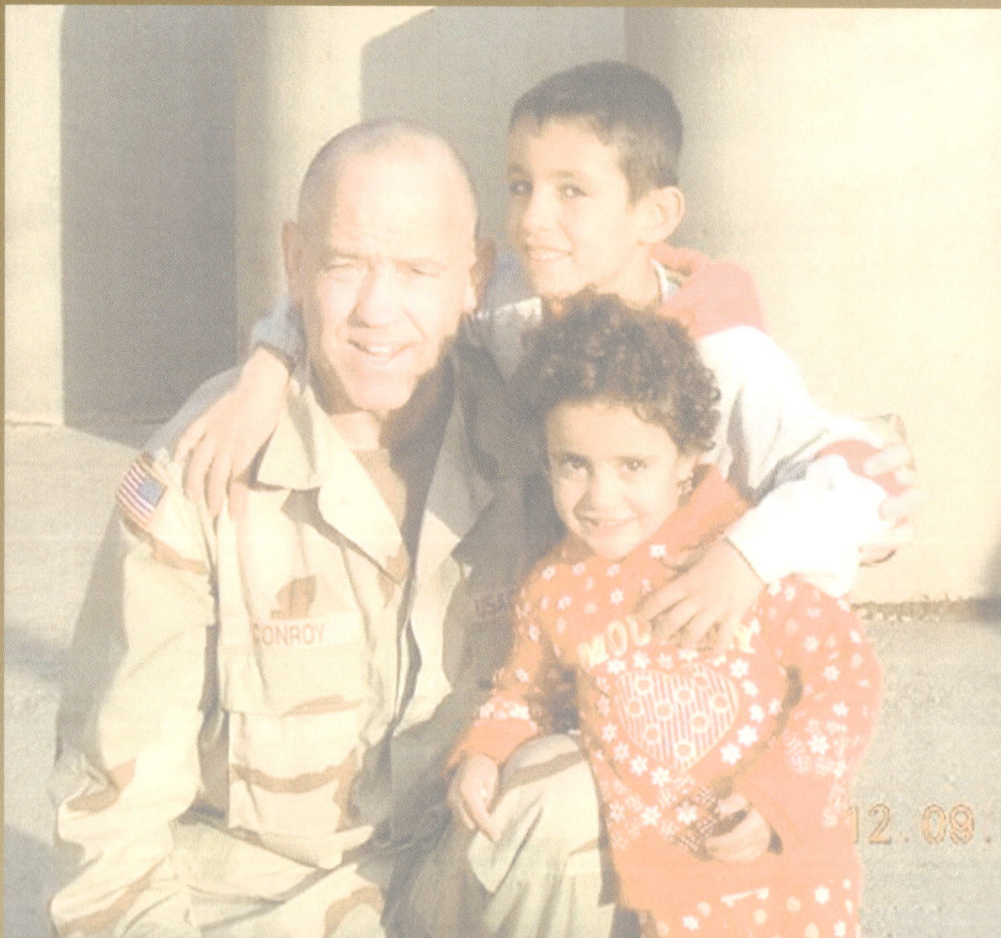

Unrelenting Line, Rocking Steady

My buddies on the left side, my AG on the right
My commander standing out front
We are all ready to fight

Ready to dig a foxhole
lay down suppressive fire if I must.
That's my buddy in the convoy, and I am his backup luck

Rock drills, battle drills, and rehearsals,
We do them all, we do it until we get it right
So we will know what to do when we get in the thick of the fight.

Two-horn blast means a herringbone.
Three blasts means attack by fire.
A constant blast means blow on through.
Four blasts means shut the back door.

The line is secure, my buddy got me covered.
Moving under fire
Where is the sniper?
Is he over watching this route?

The line will not stop.
The force will not retreat.
Infantrymen are doing the raid.
Artillerymen ready to fire.

Bayonet ready.
Steel from above.
Clear the path.
Moving to the LRP.

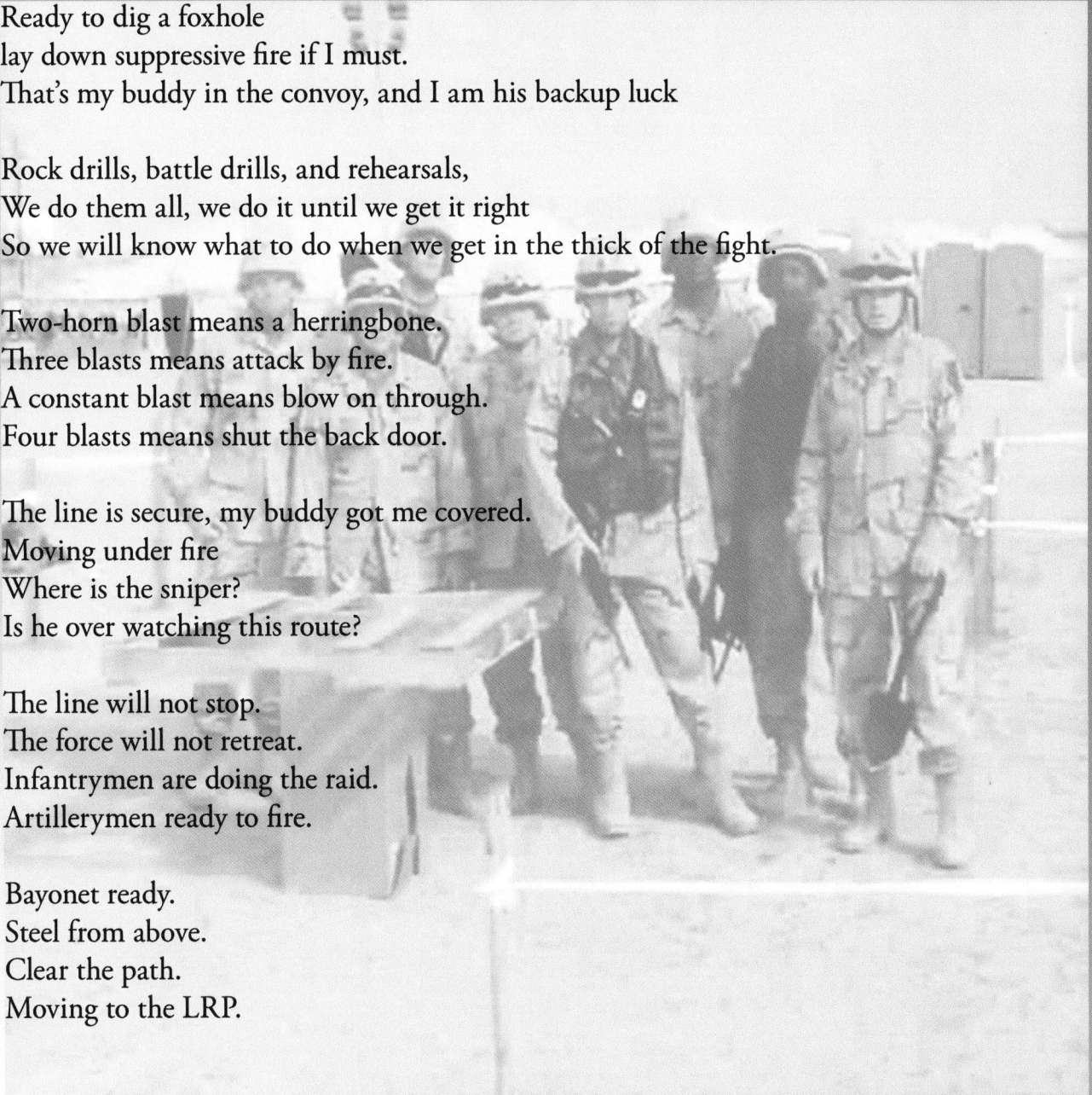

Water Flows Clean

What used to take three hours to get
 now can be had at a fingers touch
No longer waiting at the riverbanks
 now it can be had in their homes.

It is no longer a task to go get water.
It is not a scheduled event but rather a matter of moving.
Getting up and going to get what is needed.

What was once a matter of going down to the riverbanks is no longer.
It can be enjoyed with less than half the work,
expelling less than a tenth of the energy that it once did.

It flows clean and filtered.
It is cool no matter what the season
It's pure water. Water flows clean.

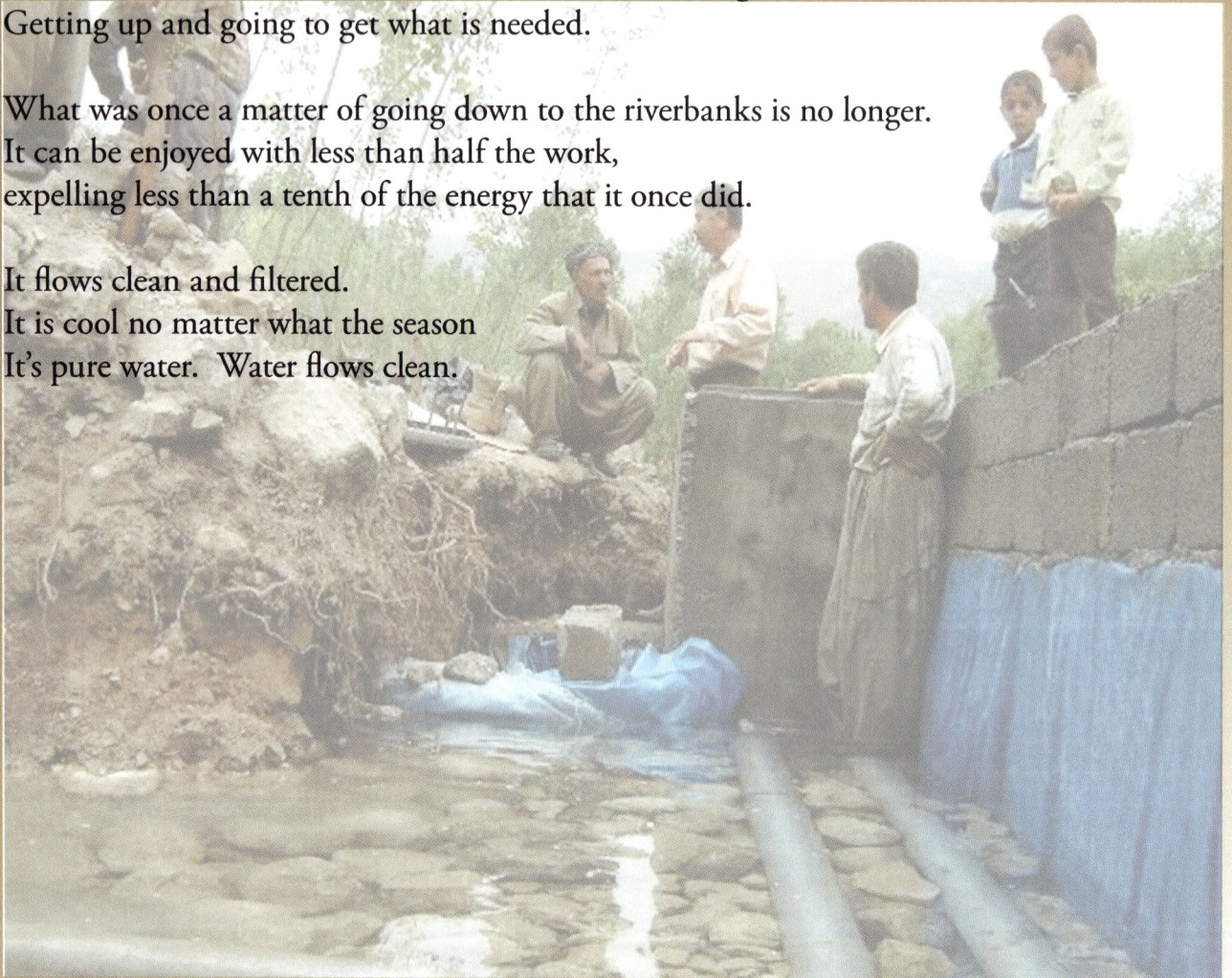

Waving What They Believe In

Everyone is on the field cheering for the buses to arrive
Mothers chanting husbands' names
Fathers chanting just the same.

Parents have their children dressed for the occasion,
to welcome love ones back from a long rugged tour.
Everyone has something to cheer about, this they know for sure.

Fathers line their kids in a row
All looking for mommy.
She is coming, can hardly wait until she exits that bus door.

And mothers dress their little girls up cute
with ponytails, bows, and ribbons galore.
Waiting for their daddy to come chasing across that grassy floor.

In all their hands is all the same thing. They all know it by name.
Its red, white and blue, and they hold it tight
Because it is the reason why mommy or daddy had to go and fight.

So there they stand on the field waiting
With a banner in their hand.
It isn't just a banner, but an emblem of a blessed land.

We All Have Our Losses

Mourning is what we all seem to do
More than we would ever like.
Weeping over love ones that we lost in some insurgent fight

VBIEDs are their weapons of choice.
Mass destruction rolling on wheels drive into a crowded area
Hear the explosions going off
And many innocents are killed.

IEDs are second best, followed by suicide bombers.
They lie in wait for the perfect gate.
They spring the trap and kill the young
The innocents who did no wrong.
Yet they call it "jihad".   I just call it bad

It's not just Americans that they have in their sights
Oh they will kill Iraqis, British, Danish and Korean alike.
And all along they call themselves right, well kiss my back.

They take away what they can never give back
So they are chasing out infidels, they are raising hell.
Every woman, man and child who loses someone
The losses are lasting and the numbers swells.

Every time a boom goes off, you read a news update.
Someone has lost another friend, son, daughter, mother or father because no one is
immune; we all have our losses.

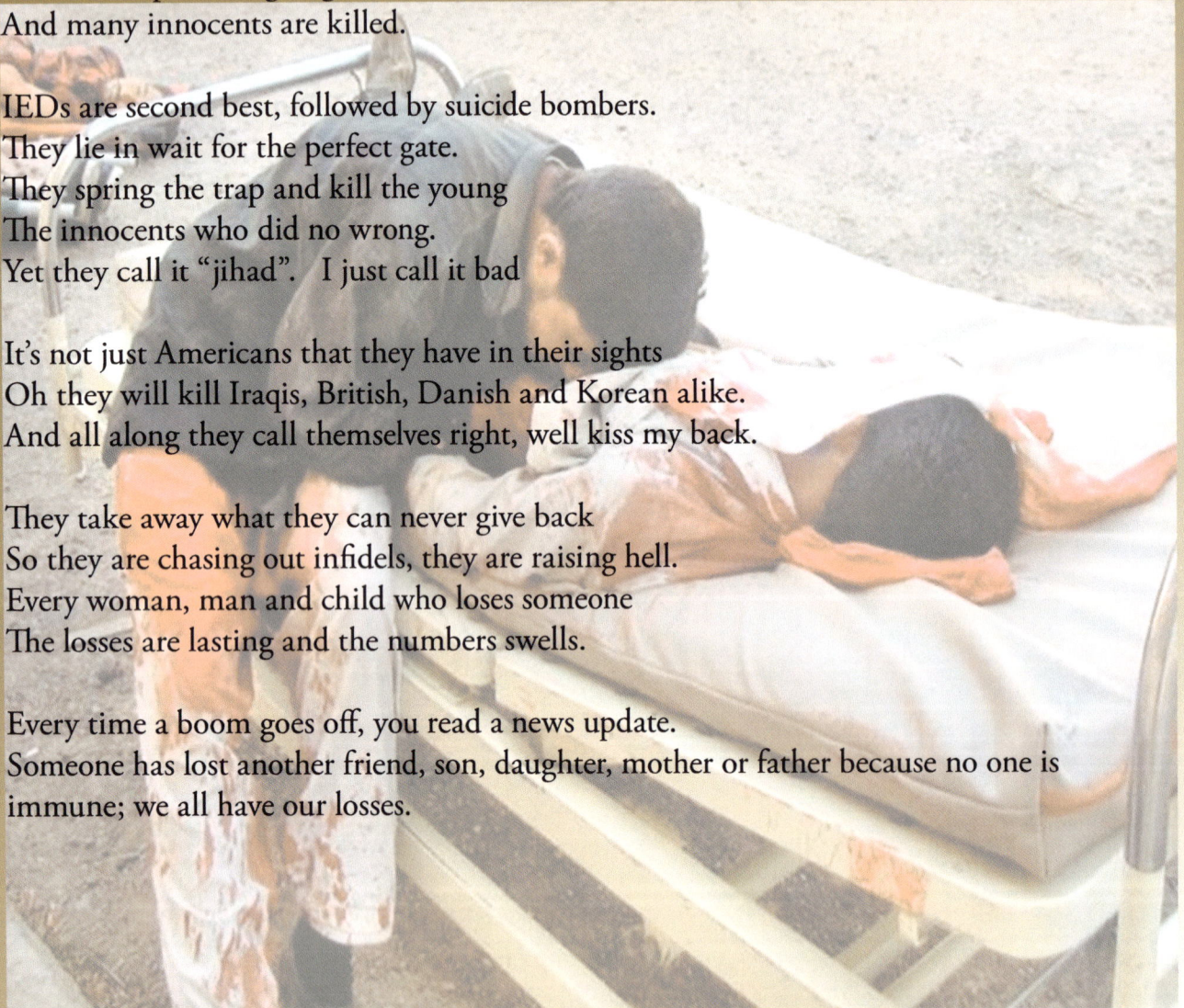

We Live Under Fire, Take Me To The Water

When the bombs started falling it was raining down hell
Shells were falling everywhere, and from where no one could tell
so we all took bunkers and hoped it would soon end
And said to one another, "If this ends, we will not sin."

It was eight rounds, no, nine rounds that fell that day.
But it was just enough to make me want to change my ways.
There had already been an IED that blew up along the road
And a VBIED that DXed a convoy truck full of class 4 load.

We lost several members that day and that should have been enough
But it took a few more mortar rounds to really shake me up.

It must have been only several feet away, but no one was hurt
Just a lot of dirt, a lot of dust but we had seen enough.
While we can't change the fire we take, the water is the best choice.
It will cleanse more than just a dirty stain.
It will cleanse a heart just the same.

So if we have to live under this fire that rains down at night
Then let the water that cleanse the soul
Be the comfort that makes me do right.

We Lost Another Brother Today

A room full of mourners all present for one purpose
At one time in one place all for the same reason
To honor one more brother, a slain relative with soaked faces.

We speak of his gallantry, his bravery, his selfless duty, and his honor.
Members of his team, his squad, and his platoon speak of his memories.
Elements of his command all gather to honor him for his service.

Each member of the family bears a burden for its lost member
All knowing that our brother has left a treasured family behind
who will never know him, that he will never see mature into adulthood.

Solemnly, we the mourners, view on a wall snapshot of our brother's life.
We see his antics, we hear his jestering, and we witness his hopes of a reunion that he will
never see, and his young child will never come to know.

Through all the reminiscing, each member present recollects something special about our
lost brother, but it is a short-lived moment.
It is then that a memorial honor is sounded, a twenty-one-gun salute, reserved for only the
valiant.

Alas, the moment arrives that we must say our parting words and
pay our last respects for one more time to one more member we have lost on a foreign soil
because we lost another brother today.

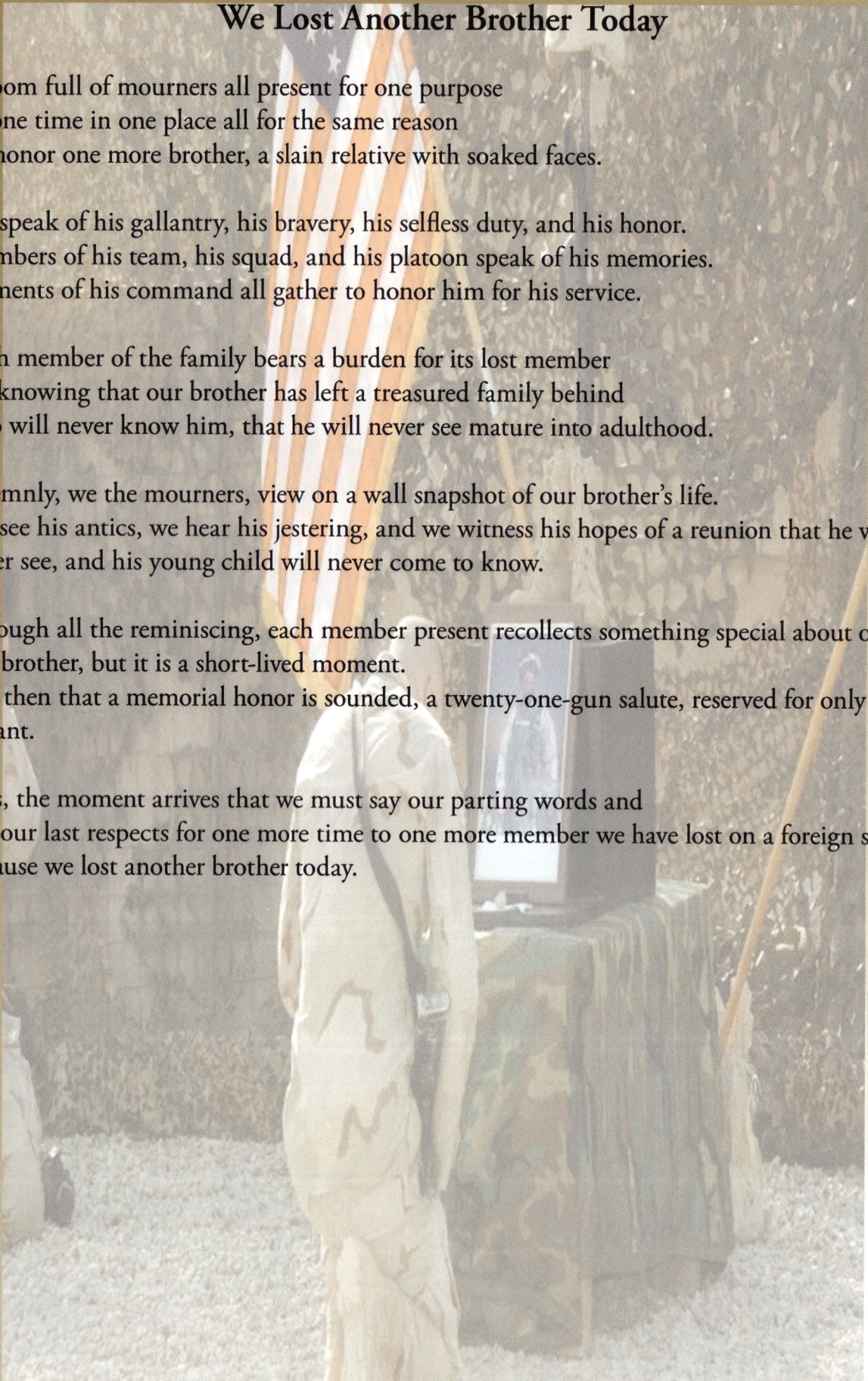

We Lost Good Friends

What seem like just a pile of rubbish and debris
Is not everything that a fellow soldier sees.
What he views is more than burnt up frames and rubber.
It's more than anything that anyone will ever see.

In the midst of the debris there are images of friends
And images of families and hope.
There are buddies who made promises and kept them.
In the wreckage there is complete mayhem.

We lost some drivers who had funny jokes
That could make anyone laugh.
There was a gunner who was a prankster that
always had a trick up his sleeve.

This wasn't just another convoy that got blown up.
It was a lot of our friends that we will never hear again.
They will not joke any more, no pranks will they pull.
It wasn't just a row of vehicles; they were our friends.

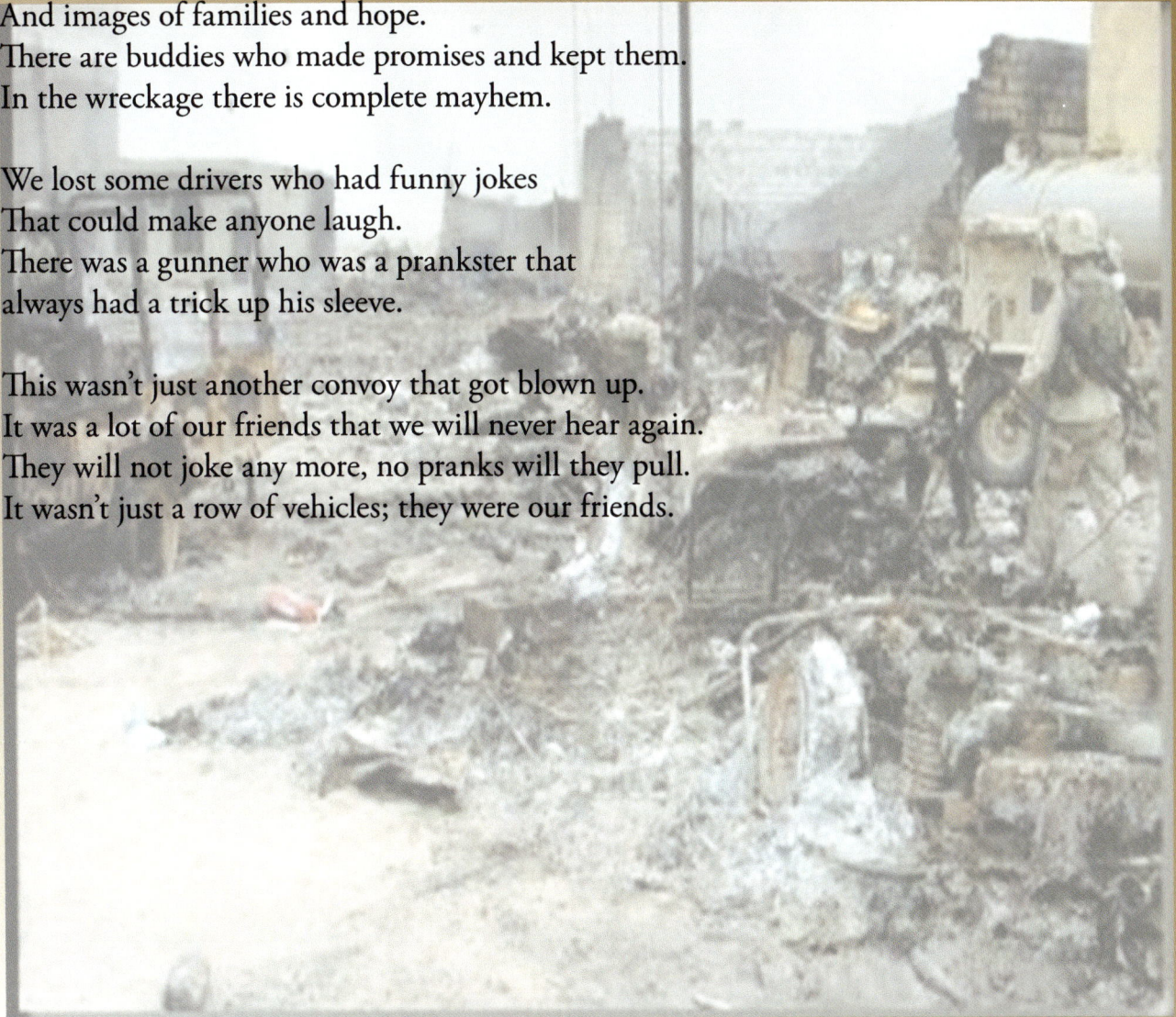

We Share The Pain

Whoever said time heals all wounds never lost a friend or better yet a leg. Time passes, but friends never come back, and a new leg never grows to replace the one amputated.

No matter how many sorrys or pats on the back that is had
No matter how many tears are shed,
The pain still lingers and nights still passes without that one soul
That one feature that made you whole.

Nothing will bring them back
No one will be just like them, know their jokes, or have that look.
Their uniqueness was what made them stand out

Only another soldier who was there knows the loss.
When we pass in familiar gatherings, we throw a glance and the other knows we care…
knowing we feel the pain they have.

A tie that is not based upon ethnicity binds us
It is not based upon gender or socio-economical backgrounds.
Our likeness is interwoven between us, based upon what we saw.

When we call each other brothers or buddies, it is not a jargon.
It is a belief, because we trusted each other like brothers and sisters.
So it is not about pretending, it is about remembering.

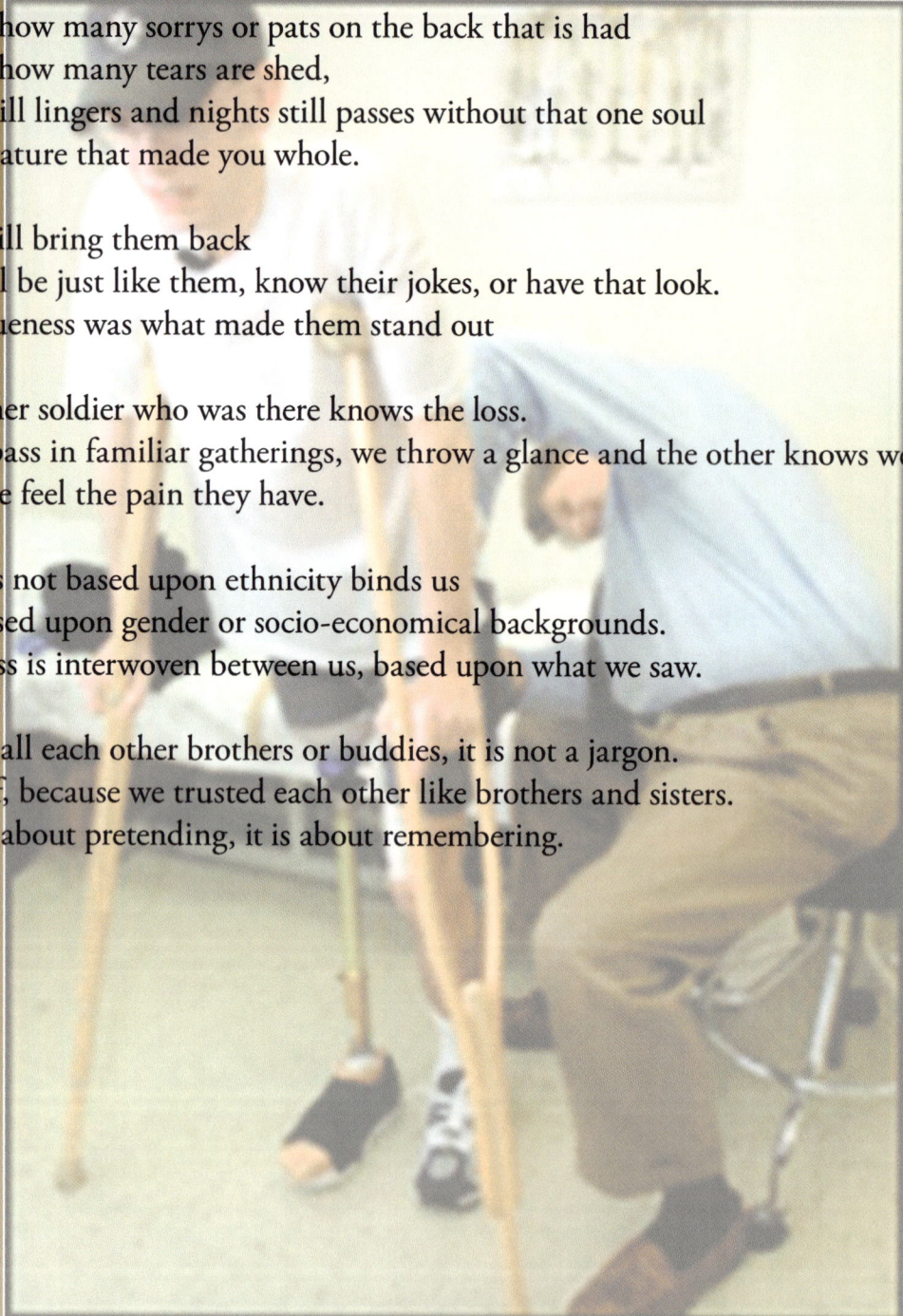

Willow Eyes With a Hopeful Smile

How adoring of an image as if to be a willow tree
A slim figure without any distinguishing glamour
With drooping limbs by her side, fixed in this moment in time.

In her petiteness she stands, a flower waiting to bloom
Eyes affixed on what is beyond her
But hoping that she will perhaps be there one day.

Her facade displays a hidden smile
Common for a willow of a child.
Yet she presents a statue that is strong
That will stand the test of trials in the midst of wrongs.

Everything that is beautiful doesn't just come into being
As a small sapling is only a foreshadow of what it shall be
An awesome image so undefined, her limitations are not had in her mind.

Willow eyes and drooping limbs say little of the hope inside.
The smile is what gives it away for what she can become one day.
Little willow with hopeful smile don't be denied
This is your life, take it all in stride.

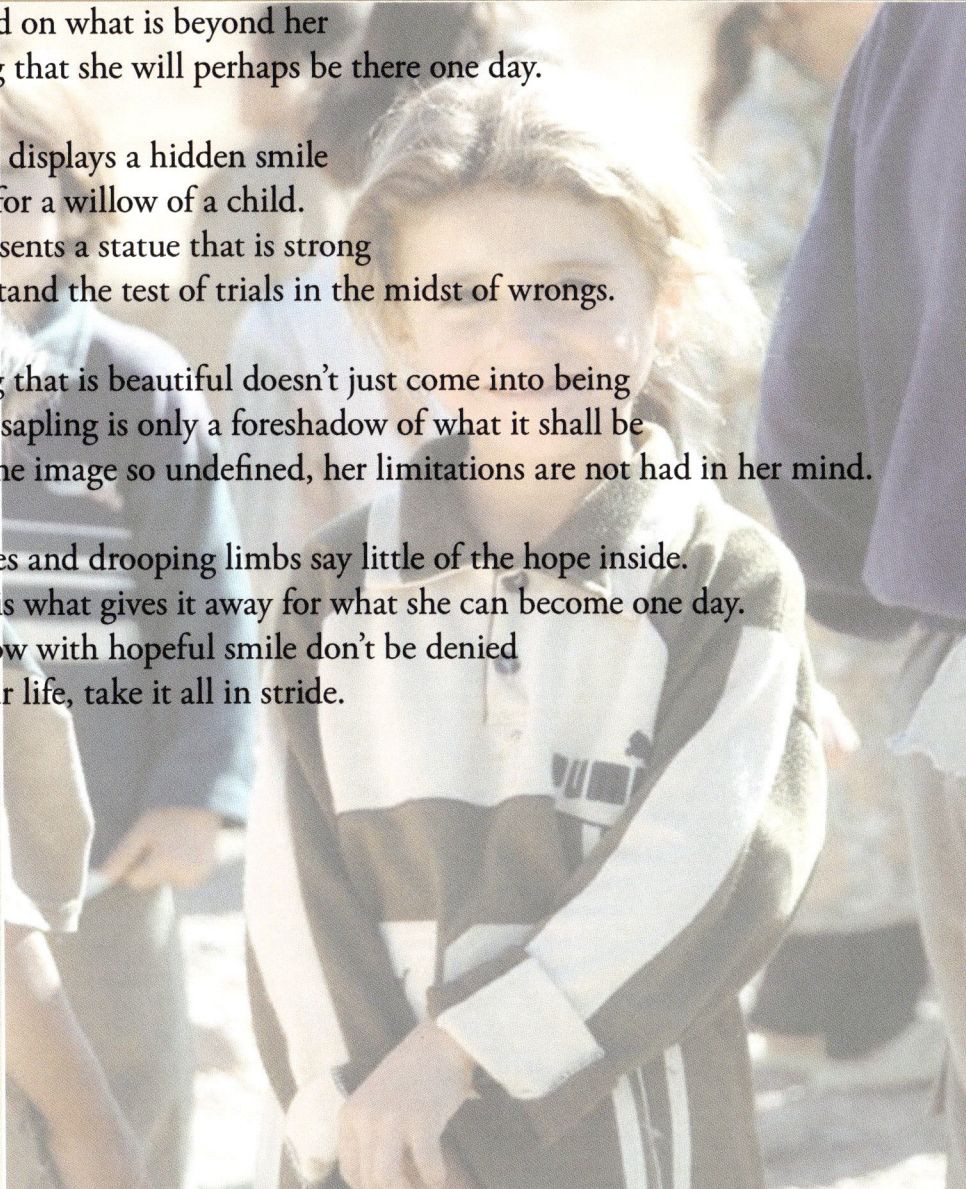

What is Said For A Passing Soldier?

There we are assembled to honor their memories
Soldiers who have given their best until the end
To their buddies they are known as friends
To those who never knew them, heroes.

We speak of their selfless sacrifice
Of the family they have left behind
Just how much of a trooper they were
And the thing that we will remember most.

We will talk of their last words
What they loved more than anything else
Just how committed they were to the mission
Just before we knew we had lost them.

We will hear his name called for one last time.
There will be no answer and hearts will fall.
Knowing they are gone was bad enough
But to hear their name and no answer is just too much.

When all pass and pay their respects
Every member there will remember something else
Something funny, something serious, something big
and something small.

Then we will leave in silence
Knowing that another soldier is out of our ranks.

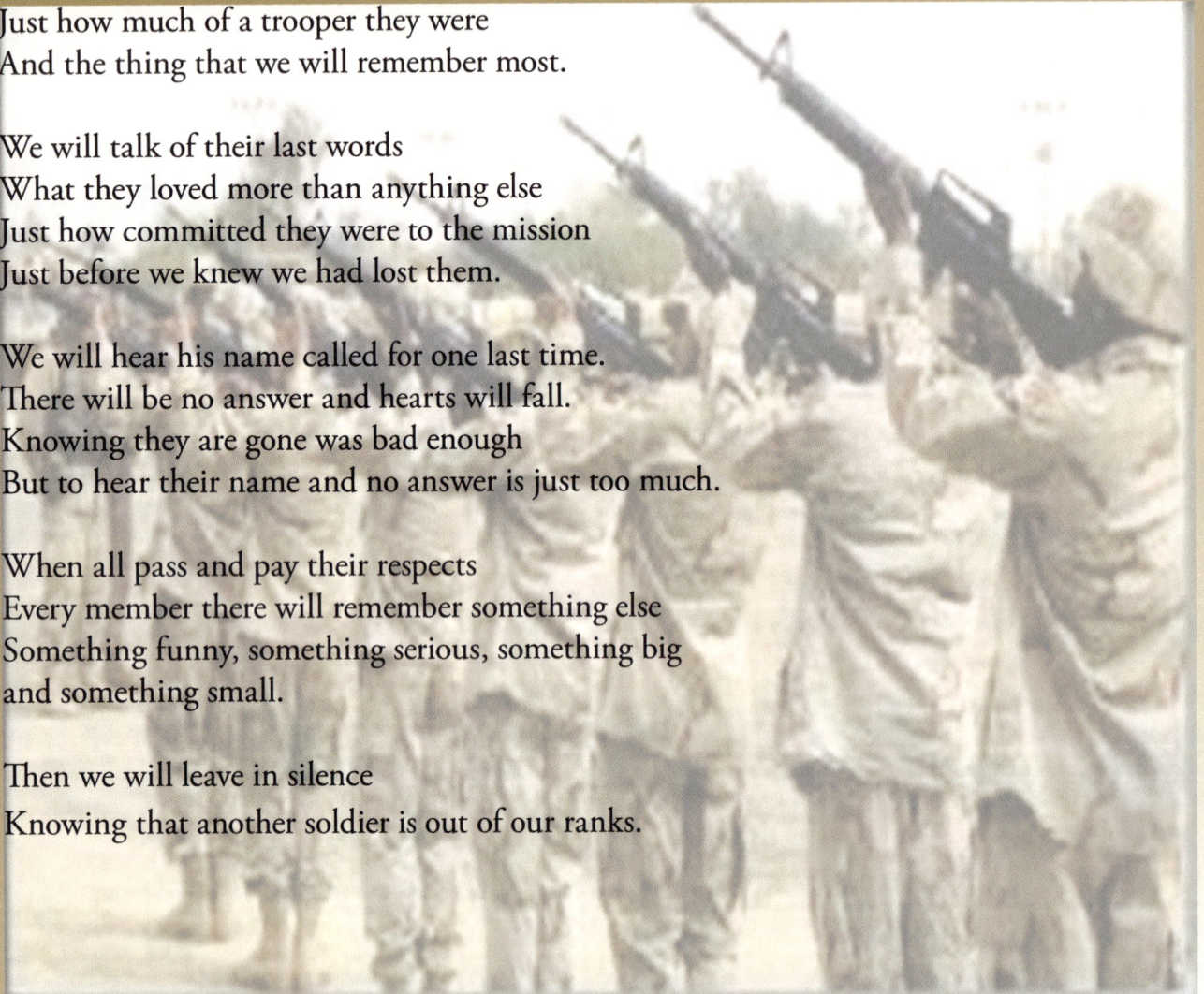

Why We Are There

Our mission is to restore democracy
Bring hope to despair
Removing the tyranny that once existed
To make the lives of the people much better than they knew before.

Although all these things are our mission
It's the looks in the eyes of little children that make it worthwhile.
For too many decades these children have had no future to look to, now they look with anticipation.

There is hope in the faces where there was grim doubt.
There is a smile where once existed a frown.
Children now express appearances of jovialness where images of depression once existed.
Their souls are changed forever.

Those eyes actually smile now.
They are alive as opposed to waiting for some dreaded fate.
With genuine expressions of happiness, they live for a tomorrow.

The papers read, "Why are soldiers being lost on the streets"?
For the soldiers on the streets, the purpose is not seen in the news.
It's the faces of hope, the smiles of possibilities and the lives changed.

If only the papers, the morning news shows saw what we saw,
there would be no doubt to our why, no question to our resolve.

The answer would be clear.

Just looking in the faces of those whose lives we have changed is enough

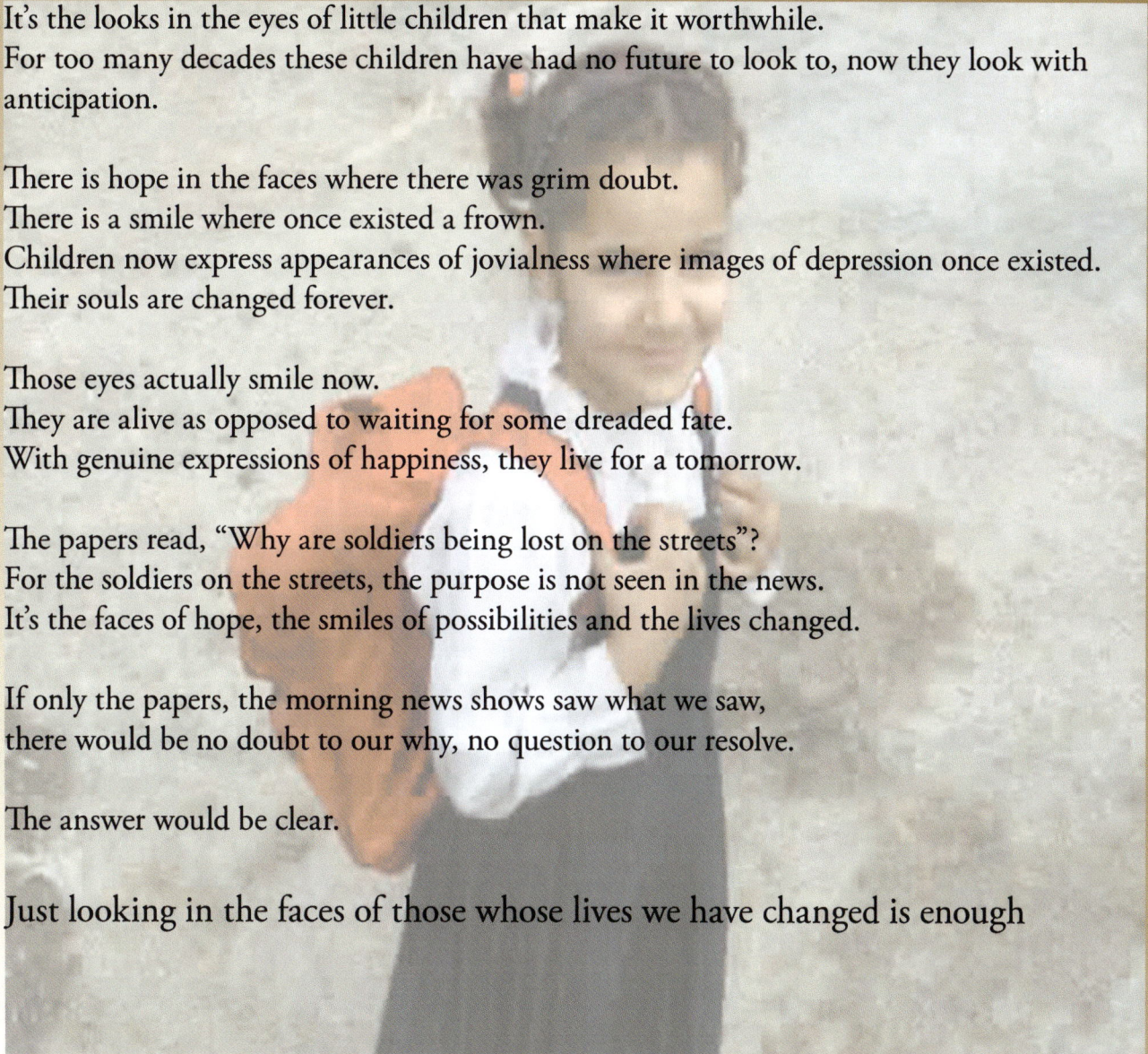

Through A Soldier's Eyes From His Heart

Danger lurks around every corner no matter where you go.
As you walk down a road to work, shrapnel may hit you,
or better yet a rocket that came over the wall.

Every friendship, every relationship, every face that you ever greet
You think to yourself, will I see them again?
Until the time that you don't see them and you wonder why.

In the middle of the night when you hear the mortars fall
and you count them off one by one
Nine rounds fired, five soldiers hit and you think to yourself
That could have been it.

You read in the news or hear in a meeting that another aircraft
just went down. How many soldiers? How are they doing?
These are the questions everyone asks.

Even worse still is when you see everyone scrambling
And you know someone has been hit.
Until you ask that strategic question and you hear the answer
You want it all to quit.

It's not just anyone, but someone that you knew.
It's a father, someone's brother, and someone's daughter
You knew them well. Water swells in your eyes as you hear them tell.

At the memorial service you meet everyone who knew them.
There is not a dry eye in the place
And the hearts are heavy as hell.

They say that time will heal the pain.
In fifty years they will still be gone.
The absence will remain the same.

Such Eyes Shouldn't See

What mayhem is scattered on the streets
Body parts that don't match, a hand and a knee.
Precious blood ran like a river
Pooling around scrambling feet.

An innocent child who was standing by saw the crash
Heard the blast, and saw the lives of many consumed
But a soldier comes to shield his eyes
Knowing inside the child is crying.

Such innocent eyes who perhaps had virtuous sight
Virtue is no more.
This child shall forever see the events
Of this horrid day when he sleeps at night.

Even when the debris is gone and water has washed away
The last evidence that this tragedy ever took place,
It will still be fresh in this child's mind.

Not only was virture taken when he saw
The mangled lives all strewed astray
He will never see simple pleasantries.
Such things such eyes should not see.

Printed in the United States
1145LVUK00001B